KCFE 63

Kingston College of Further Education

KU-693-057

WITHDRAWN
FROM
LEARNING RESOURCES
CENTRE
KINGSTON COLLEGE

Inside Staff Development

Inside Staff Development

Judy Bradley
Rosemary Chesson
Jane Silverleaf

KINGSTON COLLEGE OF FURTHER EDUCATION LIBRARY

NFER-Nelson

Published by The NFER-Nelson Publishing Company Ltd.,
Darville House, 2 Oxford Road East,
Windsor, Berks, SL4 1DF

Reprinted 1983

© NFER, 1983

ISBN   0-7005-1001-X

Code 8095 02 1

All rights reserved. No part of this publication may be
reproduced or transmitted, in any form or by any means,
without permission.

This book is sold subject to the standard conditions of
the Net Book Agreement.

Distributed in the USA by Humanities Press Inc.,
Atlantic Highlands, New Jersey 07716 USA.
Printed by The Whitefriars Press Ltd Tonbridge

Acc. No. 0 0 1 7 5 7 0 7

Class No. 370.711

Date Rec 4 11 83

Order No F 30558

Contents

Acknowledgements

We should like to express our gratitude to all those who
helped us in the course of this research. Staff in all
the colleges we visited gave up their time to complete
questionnaires and to participate in our interview programme. Without their generosity this report could not
have been produced. We should also like to thank those
representatives of the Regional Advisory Councils, local
education authorities and other agencies who helped us
considerably in placing our observations in their wider
context.

Our thanks are due to the members of our Steering
Committee, in particular the Chairman, Dr George Tolley,
for advice and encouragement throughout the project.

Finally, our special thanks go to Christine Negus whose
efficiency, accuracy and patience throughout the research
have contributed in no small measure to the preparation
of this report.

JB
RC
JS
March, 1981

List of items and tables

CHAPTER 1

Introduction

During the 1950s and 60s when further education was enjoying a period of rapid expansion very little thought was given to staff development. There were few opportunities within the vast recruitment drive to ensure that staff were fully prepared for the teaching roles they were to perform, while the relative ease of advancement meant that individuals often found themselves in senior posts with no training in, or experience of, college management. By the mid-1970s the situation had changed drastically. Financial restrictions and fluctuations in educational demand meant that staff were faced with severely reduced prospects for promotion and even with the threat of redundancy. At the same time they were being asked to possess a more varied range of professional skills to meet the demands being made by the introduction of new types of course and by the students following them.

The growth of staff development

In 1978 a policy statement from NATFHE expressed the view that: 'Many of the urgent specific and long-term problems currently facing further and higher education would have been reduced if there had been a systematic pattern of teacher education for this area' (NATFHE, 1978, p3). At the time it was a well publicized fact that two-thirds of the FE teaching force had received no initial teacher training. However, the first step towards remedying this had already been taken. Following a report from the Advisory Committee for the Supply and Training of Teachers, DES Circular 11/77 recommended the introduction of systematic arrangements for an increase in initial and post-experience training, with priority being placed on the induction of new staff.

The publication of Circular 11/77 had an interesting

1

effect with regard to staff development. While on the one hand providing an undoubted impetus in initial training, it tended to divert attention from other areas of need. Much of the concern about the development of staff now centred on enhancing their skills as teachers, and the majority of schemes adopted this as their primary focus. This is perhaps understandable, since classroom teaching is the most common activity engaged upon in the colleges. However, it has often meant that the concept of staff development has been taken to imply solely initial training or course attendance. Indeed in a significant number of colleges this view prevails, while the facilities for other kinds of provision continue to be underexploited.

The NATFHE statement referred to earlier pointed out that initial training should be seen as only one part – albeit a fundamental one – in a continuing programme of professional development for the individual teacher. New techniques would be needed if colleges were to address the challenges presented by the 1980s. These might entail: retraining for new high demand subjects or to meet the needs of the young unemployed; secondment and release to industry and commerce; planned changes of responsibility for course design, student selection and short course organization; regular opportunities to undertake research or consultancy; and exchange teaching visits to enable staff to approach their work from a new perspective. Management, too, is an area in which further education must take steps both to catch up with the past and to provide for current and future training needs. It must also be expected that career counselling will take on an increasingly important role. Staff development embraces all of these.

There are, of course, certain aspects of a development programme which are only feasible with a reasonable degree of centralization. However, the ACSTT subcommittee clearly held the view that: 'There is likely to be an advantage in making staff training and development a normal and lively activity in each institution rather than something that is provided only from external sources' (ACSTT, 1975, p14). This focussing of attention on college responsibility for staff development echoed the opinion expressed in the influential report produced by the ACFHE/APTI Working Party (1973). This document made a number of practical recommendations regarding the implementation of a broader concept of development and was greeted with considerable interest, numerous colleges taking the guidelines offered therein as a basis from which to build up their own schemes. In

2

recent years, however, there has been some resistance
within colleges to the whole idea of staff development.
This appears to spring from the notion that the active
pursuit of development activities on the part of the
individual was a means of achieving promotion. The view
that staff development has a particularly important role
to play in a period of restricted prospects is by no
means universally held within the FE sector as a whole.
The fact that the resistance is essentially passive
makes it no less difficult to overcome.

Further education staff who remain committed to the
vital importance of the enterprise have themselves set
about establishing a framework for the exchange of ideas
on current issues in staff development. The Standing
Conference on Educational Development in Polytechnics
(SCEDSIP) has, since its inception in 1974, organized
workshops and published a series of occasional papers
and newsletters designed to disseminate news of forthcoming events and to provide brief descriptions of
existing staff development programmes. This initiative
was soon followed by the establishment of the National
Association for Staff Development (NASD), the Southern
and West Midlands Staff Development Networks, and a
variety of other regional and local groups. The aim of
all of these groups is essentially to provide support
for people previously working in isolation and to build
a forum for the discussion of all aspects of policy and
practice. In addition there are specialist organizations,
such as the Association of Professional Tutors, which
serve a similar function for their members. Thus, while
the co-ordination of activities on a national or regional
level is only just beginning to be considered on any
significant scale, informal communication channels are
emerging which will undoubtedly prove to be of major importance in determining the future of staff development.

Defining staff development

The first issue of the Southern Network's Staff Development Newsletter began with the words: 'The idea of staff
development in further education has reached an uncomfortable stage in its growth. It has passed through the
difficult years of establishing its existence and its
importance, but is still confused rather than coherent...
unsure of its own nature and uncertain of its proper
direction' (1977, p1). Certainly clear agreement as to
the nature of staff development has yet to be achieved
in spite of the deliberations of numerous committees,
working parties and individuals. The task of providing
a definition is made difficult by the necessity to do

3

justice to its wide diversity. In the event the very
comprehensiveness of the definitions that have emerged
means, as Hewton (1980) has remarked, that one is uncertain where normal organizational activity ends and
staff development begins.

The most commonly cited definition is that offered by
Warren Piper and Glatter (1977): 'a systematic attempt
to harmonise individuals' interests and wishes, and
their carefully assessed requirements for furthering
their careers with the forthcoming requirements of the
organization within which they are expected to work'
(p25). The potential conflict between the needs and
wishes of individuals and the demands of the organization means that putting such a definition into practice
is fraught with political complications. Essentially
the debate centres on the question of who is to carry
out this careful assessment of requirements. Although
it must be regarded as lying at the heart of any coherent
development programme, this question has not generally
been answered in a way that is satisfactory to all
concerned.

Colleges have traditionally been characterized by a
fairly rigid chain of command with the principal
dominating decisions at the policy level, but having
little control over staff in relation to the act of
teaching. Early forays into the staff development arena
tended to retain the overall framework of management
control, while attempting to extend it into an area
where the classroom teacher had held individual autonomy.
The document produced by the ACFHE/APTI Working Party may
be seen as representative of this 'management' model:
'... staff development looks at the teacher's various
functions inside his college, at his strengths and weaknesses, at his present and future roles, and then,
having assessed his requirements, seeks to meet them.
It also carefully considers the teacher in relation to
the college in which he works in order that possible
conflicts between personal development and college development may be avoided. So...we define staff development
as identifying the professional needs of individual
teachers and devising programmes to meet those needs'
(ACFHE/APTI, 1973, p4). It was made quite clear that
staff development was the responsibility of management,
that the identification of needs was to be carried out
by senior staff members, and that teachers who were unwilling to accept a management definition of the situation were to be cajoled or coerced into participating:
'It is possible that some teachers in colleges may object
to pressure being put on them to take part in training

4

programmes to meet needs either diagnosed or thought
necessary by their seniors.... We feel this is a view
that management cannot accept under the present circumstances (or, indeed, under any set of circumstances) and
must seek to change'(Ibid, p7).

Superimposed on this situation is the growing movement
towards the democratization of the colleges whereby
teachers would play a much greater part in the decision-
making process. From the point of view of staff development a self-initiated approach has been demanded in
which management would play an essentially non-directive,
supportive role. Sayer and Harding (1974), for instance,
argue that, 'Those involved in staff development can
seek to help individual teachers make their own peculiar
adaptive relationships to the particular situation they
find themselves in by aiding and abetting definition of
their own goals and priorities within their own talents
and interests, their own best methods of operation'.
These writers talk of a process of 'encouraging
constructive doubt'.

Staff development schemes currently operating within the
further education sector tend to have reached an uncomfortable compromise between these two approaches. In
what has come to be known as the 'partnership model'
there is an implied commitment by the individual to the
achievement of institutional objectives and by management to the removal of constraints against individual
interests. In reality this is difficult to achieve, and
unfortunately has often resulted in ambiguous or ill-
defined statements of policy, particularly with regard
to the assessment of needs and the roles and responsibilities of individual members of staff, including those
with designated responsibility for the development of
their colleagues. Because of this ambiguity and the
cover-all nature of definitions, some colleges can
delude others - and sometimes even themselves - into
believing that they are in the vanguard of the staff
development enterprise. One of the first things to come
to our notice when embarking on this investigation was
the fact that schemes which look very impressive on
paper can often amount to little more than a list of
intentions that have never come to fruition.

The current state of the art can perhaps best be characterized as small-scale activity on the part of enthusiastic groups of individuals whose commitment and sustained efforts have produced rational and responsive
schemes for their own colleges, despite the absence of
active support from the FE system as a whole. Further

5

education prides itself on its diversity and the guidelines which emerge from this report are not therefore
intended as blueprints or checklists of good practice.
Rather they are ideas which we hope will stimulate reflection and action. A staff development scheme con-
tributes to the maintenance and growth of a specific
set of values endorsed by the college as an institution,
as a group of interacting individuals. Each college
must, then, focus attention on its own critical problems
and special circumstances and select the solutions and
strategies most appropriate to them.

Research design

The project began in July 1978 with the aims of identifying the current and possible future needs of teaching
staff in the further education sector; assessing how far
these were being met by existing schemes; and outlining
successful strategies currently in operation. Our
objective has been to investigate the complexities of
staff development in practice and to examine underlying
questions about policy and implementation that are of
concern to those involved.

Our first requirement was a broad base of information
which would enable us to build up a picture of the
nature and range of development opportunities being
offered within the sector as a whole. Some information
on current thinking at the regional level was already
available from the reports made to the DES by the regional advisory councils in response to Circular 11/77.
RACs provided the research team with copies of these
reports. In order to obtain more detailed data on individual colleges in each region, the team spent the
early months of the project visiting further education
institutions throughout England and Wales. At this exploratory stage we sought advice from as many different
sources as possible regarding any local or regional
initiatives that might be of interest. Members of HMI
provided us with lists of colleges in their areas of
responsibility which appeared to have adopted interesting
approaches to staff development and discussions were held
with representatives of national groups such as the NASD
and NATFHE. These, together with our own previous experience of researching into the further education sector
suggested numerous locations for our initial visits.
During each of these college visits all relevant documentation was collected and discussions were held with
senior staff and with professional tutors or staff
development officers.

On the basis of these visits twenty colleges representing a variety of successful approaches to staff development and demonstrating a number of the difficulties involved were chosen for detailed investigation. In
selecting this group several additional factors were
taken into consideration - size of college, organizational structure, geographical location, availability of
financial resources - all of which can act as constraints
on the implementation of an effective scheme. All of
the colleges chosen had a high proportion of non-advanced
work, though in certain of them staff are expected to
teach across the entire range. The pace of innovation
and change at the non-advanced level has in recent years
been particularly marked, and it was expected that
further education colleges would be heavily involved in
creating structures and processes to meet the new external demands being placed on them.

The data to be reported in later chapters were collected
using a variety of procedures including observation,
interviews, group discussions, questionnaires and the
content analysis of college documents. Any kind of
survey approach, relying heavily on the use of questionnaires, was for several reasons not considered to be an
appropriate strategy. Firstly, it was necessary for us
to determine the key issues to be examined since there
has been so little previous research in this area to
indicate what these might be. We were very conscious
of the fact that by prestructuring the investigation we
could run the risk of concentrating on those aspects of
staff development which prove easy to measure, with the
attendant consequence that these would come to be
identified with those which are valuable to measure.
Secondly, the level of consistency necessary for the
use of a survey design could not be assumed for staff
development provision. Heavy reliance on structured
questionnaire data was moreover precluded by the existence of conflicting values, imprecise definitions,
few agreed-upon assessment criteria, and the differential
use of terminology, all of which characterize the current
literature on our subject. Thirdly, the effects of
schemes and the difficulties involved in their implementation are not readily apparent. One could collect
statistics, for example, on course attendance, and point
to the number of staff served but this would not advance
the research very far, since it immediately raises the
question of establishing criteria for assessing the relative merits of quantity and quality of different types
of staff development activity. Evidence of the real
impact of staff development schemes tends to be too
elusive and ambiguous for such a narrow approach.

7

Having selected a group of colleges for detailed investigation, our first task was to incorporate as many different viewpoints as possible to represent the different interests within each institution. This phase of the research therefore began with the design of unstructured questionnaires. In addition to the information gained from our initial round of discussions, pilot studies were carried out to ensure that the questions would be both relevant and comprehensible. We wished to avoid imposing artificial constraints, preferring to identify those issues in staff development which were of concern to FE staff themselves. These issues were then subjected to more intensive and sustained examination at interview.

In March 1979 open-ended questionnaires were sent to the principals of the twenty selected colleges. They covered a number of issues that had arisen from our early informal discussions and enabled us to gain an overall view of the history, growth and possible future of staff development within each institution and of some of the assumptions underlying policy and practice in this area. An additional open-ended questionnaire to all heads of department provided information on the practicalities of implementing college policy at the departmental level, together with heads' own experiences of development and the nature of their involvement in their college's staff development scheme. One of the colleges was regrettably forced to withdraw from the research as its buildings had been severely damaged by fire and any additional demands made on staff would have been unwelcome. It was decided not to attempt to replace it with another institution. All of the remaining nineteen principals completed their questionnaires. Of the 149 questionnaires sent out to heads of department 77 (52 per cent) were returned.

During April 1979 a questionnaire was sent to all full-time teaching staff in the participating colleges. The numbers involved ruled out the possibility of using a completely open-ended instrument. Pre-coded questions were therefore included in cases where response sets were already known - such as grade, age, sex, education and qualifications - the open-ended format being retained for items where experiences might be expected to differ and reactions to be unpredictable. Respondents were encouraged also to take up points not explicitly covered in the questionnaire and to comment fully on matters of current concern regarding their professional situation. The vast majority of respondents did in fact use this opportunity to provide us with detailed informa-

8

tion on their own experiences of staff development schemes and to indicate additional areas of interest. 1,217 completed questionnaires were returned by the cut-off date representing 29 per cent of the original mailing. Although this response rate was disappointingly low, it did not disrupt the logical development of the project since the data obtained by this method were regarded as a starting point for further investigation rather than an end in themselves. It may, however, be of interest to note that the grade and sex of respondents closely matched the distributions within the nineteen colleges and the FE population in general.

In order to ascertain whether there might be a relationship between attitudes to and experience of staff development and the response to our research, non-respondents were included in our later interview programme. These interviews indicated that the respondents to the questionnaire were in fact representative of staff within the selected colleges. In particular, there was nothing to suggest that those who had responded were teachers who held especially favourable or unfavourable opinions of staff development or who had availed themselves of particular kinds of development opportunity. The interviews also enabled us to obtain information on reasons for non-response. As well as the common explanations of inertia and pressure of work, it was of interest to discover that a further reason lay in the view that staff development has little relevance in a time of decreased mobility and financial cutbacks. Overall, areas of consensus and divergence on a wide range of issues emerged from the questionnaire responses, which provided us with a broad base of material to be followed up in the next stage of field work.

In September 1979, we began a series of intensive case studies in six of the participating colleges. In every case the colleges were extremely welcoming and helpful to us. No restrictions were placed on our attendance at meetings, the questions we might ask or the individuals we might approach. We were given access to all policy statements and other documentation relevant to staff development, and staff themselves were unstinting in the amount of time they were prepared to devote to participating in our interview programme as well as to informal discussions. The pattern of work for each case study entailed the use of a variety of research techniques during each of our extended visits to the colleges. Members of the team carried out observations of relevant committees at work, such as the staff development committee, heads of departments' committee and the

9

Academic Board, and were given access to documentation relating to the past and current concerns of the committees together with their terms of reference. The observations were of particular value in enabling us to contextualize remarks made by staff concerning the structure, function and effectiveness of these various bodies.

While we took every opportunity to hold informal discussions with members of staff, the greatest part of each visit to the college was devoted to a series of one-to-one interviews with staff at all levels and in all departments. All staff of head of department status and above were interviewed, since their views might be expected to have particular influence over the development of their more junior colleagues. All staff with designated responsibility for staff development were interviewed. At least one interview was held with seven principals (one college had undergone a change of principal during the course of the investigation), nine vice-principals, 46 heads of department, and 196 (15 per cent) of staff at other grades. In certain cases a second interview was held in order to clarify issues arising during the course of the interview programme or in the light of evidence emerging from later visits to the college in question. This interview material was the major source of information on attitudes, opinions and experiences of the policy and practice of staff development reported in later chapters. It should, however, be stressed that the entire interview programme for the research included interviews which were carried out as part of the earlier phases of field work, and this too has been drawn upon. In total, one-to-one interviews were held with 364 further education staff members.

All interviews were unstructured, being centred on a variety of topics rather than on specific sets of questions. We considered this approach to be essential if we were to go beyond the kind of information available from policy statements and the like. It allowed us to discover that the views of those responsible for the development of their colleagues by no means always coincide with a scheme's stated objectives; while privately expressed expectations and attitudes can differ significantly from publicly stated opinions at every level within a college. The political sensitivity of some of the issues raised – sources of resistance and barriers to implementation were often attributed to interpersonal relations and the incompetence or lack of interest of specific individuals – further reinforced our conviction

10

that a highly structured schedule would have been of extremely limited value.

Reference has already been made to the fact that liaison between the research team and the regional advisory councils began at a very early stage of the project. All RACs and the six LEAs responsible for our final group of colleges were approached again early in 1980 with questionnaires seeking information on regional and local initiatives in and attitudes towards staff development. Completed questionnaires were received from all regional advisory councils and from the local authorities. Where necessary, follow-up interviews were carried out to clarify and expand the data obtained.

Throughout the research process attempts were made to elicit audience feedback from the identification of important issues to the preparation of the final report. At various stages discussions were held, for example with representatives of the NASD, the Southern and West Midlands Staff Development Networks, the Association of Professional Tutors, the institutions providing FE teacher training courses, the FE Staff College, the Council for Educational Technology, a number of RAC working parties, the Further Education Curriculum Review and Development Unit and other researchers working on a variety of aspects of staff development. A meeting of professional tutors and others with major responsibility for staff development who were participating in our study was held at the NFER after the first phase of field work. This proved to be particularly useful in clarifying issues of current concern, and in enabling participants to exchange ideas on particular approaches to their work, to discuss common problems and to discover how others were working towards a solution. Towards the end of the project, conferences covering a variety of topics arising from our study were held. Thus, although detailed data were collected from a relatively small number of colleges, we were able to carry out checks that our evidence had a much wider applicability within the further education sector as a whole.

The principal sources of comments in the text are the open-ended questionnaire responses, the group discussion material and, particuarly, the unstructured interview material obtained from staff in all the colleges we visited during the course of the research. Unless otherwise stated, the attribution of views to 'several', 'many' and other such terms merely avoids the constant repetition of 'the majority'. This is not meant to imply that consensus alone can accord a particular view any

11

absolute validity. Sometimes a point can be illuminated by the special perspective of one person. Where such an individual is quoted this is made apparent in the text. Where possible, staff who participated in our investigation speak for themselves. While we may not necesarily endorse all the opinions expressed - and where this is the case it is made clear in the text - it is the researcher's responsibility to report them. The use of illustrative quotations offers evidence in a way that is more direct and self-evident in its implications than the narration of observed incidents or second-hand opinions. It enables us to present actual responses alongside our own interpretations and evaluations of the issues which comprise the complexity of staff development in action.

CHAPTER 2

Staff development policies

One of the aims of this investigation was to encourage
people within the further education sector to consider
the experience of others in devising policies for staff
development. While it is almost certainly the case that
policies designed to be operative in one institution are
not directly transferable to another, there are principles apparent in policy documents which do apply in a
wide range of contexts. Thirteen of the colleges
participating in our study have formal policy documents
concerning staff development matters. While there are
inevitable differences in emphasis and approach, a
number of common elements can be identified which take
us some way towards an understanding of the values and
assumptions underlying current institutional perceptions
of the concept of staff development. Limitations of
space naturally prevent us from including all thirteen
policy documents in this report. Two of them are reproduced here (see Items 2.1 and 2.2) to serve as examples of the ways in which different colleges have
approached the formulation of their policies in this
area. This chapter will describe the kinds of item
typically included in policy documents, and demonstrate
some of the assumptions and values they embody. Thus it
will also provide an indication of the issues to be
covered later in the report.

External influences

In the initial questionnaire sent to principals there
was a request to outline the factors influencing the
introduction of a staff development scheme into their
respective colleges, whether or not this had been accompanied by a formal policy document. A restructuring
of further education provision within the local authority, including expansions, contractions, mergers and
changes in the nature of local demand - often creating

an urgent need for retraining programmes - were commonly
mentioned. The need to ensure a more efficient use of
resources in a period of economic stringency was also
seen as influential, as were the demands made by the developments emanating from TEC, BEC, YOP and UVP schemes.
In many instances principals' responses supported the
comment made by one of the professional tutors that the
staff development programme in his college had 'growed
like Topsy', suggesting that many of the initiatives
that have taken place have been in response to a particular need felt at a particular point in time. The
fairly recent increase in demand for initial teacher
training is perhaps the most obvious example, and indeed
the Haycocks Report (1975) was frequently cited in this
context.

The nature of specific influences naturally varied according to the length of time that a given scheme has
been in operation. Some principals, for example, gave
the James Report (1972) as a catalyst, while others
cited the report of the ACFHE/APTI Working Party (1973),
and still others traced the growth of staff development
in their colleges - albeit under another name - to a
period before the publication of either of these documents. Pioneering work by individual colleges can also
act as an important external influence. Three of the
staff development programmes included in our study have
in fact been used as models by other colleges wishing to
introduce a similar scheme for their own staff. There
are, of course, problems in carrying out an exercise of
this nature since all policy documents are essentially
tailored to the requirements of a particular college
and should not be imposed as a complete 'package' on to
a new situation. There are lessons to be learned and
potentially useful ideas to be gleaned from existing
documentation which should be used as a starting point
to assist in the formulation of new individualized
policies.

Internal initiatives

Principals were also asked to indicate any initiatives
emanating from inside the college which led to the
creation of its staff development programme. Reference
was frequently made to the interest shown by a specific
individual and, indeed, during the course of our later
interviews with staff at all levels programmes would be
described as the 'brainchild' of these key individuals.
In ten of the nineteen colleges the initial move came
from the principal and in a further three from a vice-
principal. In the majority of these cases the respons-

ibility for the continued oversight and running of the programme had now been delegated. Heads of department emerged as the catalysts in two of the colleges, while in the remaining four, mention was made of groups of staff without reference to specific individuals. This is not to suggest that pressure from the grass roots was not brought to bear, but rather that initiatives appear to be more likely to succeed if they have a powerful advocate in the upper echelons of the college.

Roles and responsibilities

The responsibility for producing and updating documentation relating to staff development matters rests in the majority of colleges with committees who are themselves ultimately responsible to the Academic Board. In the context of the present concerns it is of interest to note that no relationship was found between the type of body or individual responsible for producing documentation and the type of policy statement made by the college. Where a specifically designated staff development committee exists, its composition and terms of reference are sometimes included in the overall policy document, but more often constitute a separate document. As will be shown in Chapter 3, these documents vary in the extent to which really detailed guidelines are given to help members in fulfilling their role. This may, however, be seen as symptomatic of a more fundamental problem: the attempt to avoid interpersonal conflict by failing to be sufficiently precise about policy implications. Ambiguities concerning the roles, functions, responsibilities and limits of power exercised by staff at different levels are indicative of the tendency to adopt a piecemeal approach to staff development rather than create new structures and processes as part of a coherent whole. This is perhaps most clearly reflected in the general confusion surrounding the roles to be played by heads of department and by professional tutors, particularly in relation to the ambivalance between active intervention and non-directive support. In one college, for example, the professional tutor commented: 'I have embarrassed the governors by suggesting that there should be a general policy concerning my work. In general they simply hope that it will happen rather than laying down guidelines in terms of the college's future development'.

In the case of heads of department, again policy implications for their role are rarely clarified, other than in terms of the requirement that they prepare an annual report concerning the staff development needs of their respective departments. This might include, for example, indications of where a retirement will leave a vacancy and where an existing member of staff could be trained to fill the vacant post; where there is inadequate cover for specialist work; where a new element of work needs development; and where new courses are proposed which will require further study, qualifications or experience on the part of departmental staff members. In all colleges they are required to comment on the suitability of applications made by members of their staff. They therefore constitute a very powerful influence within the staff development programme of any college. It may nevertheless be asked whether the published guidelines concerning their role are sufficiently detailed. The amount of discretion left open to heads means that we often found significant differences of interpretation and hence implementation between departments in the same college. Despite trends towards alternative organizational structures, many colleges are still highly departmentalized and our observations would tend to support the point made by Ebbutt and Brown (1978) that heads often see themselves in a paternalistic role while their staff sometimes feel that their interests are being neither considered nor defended. Where heads of department are strongly committed to the policy and practice of staff development such problems may not arise; it is, however, the case that some heads can feel their role threatened by what they regard not as rational integration but as bureaucratic centralization. In such cases they tend to reject certain of the opportunities provided within the college's programme as of little value to their staff.

The range of opportunities

A great deal about a college's interpretation of the concept of staff development can be learned from an examination of the range of opportunities offered and the areas on which greatest emphasis is placed. While certain constraints may operate according to the structure of the institution and the availability of the necessary funding, it is nevertheless of interest to outline the kinds of opportunities found in colleges in our study. Opportunities are generally broken down in policy statements into categories of 'direct' and 'indirect'. Although interpretations vary even here, direct methods usually include taught courses of induction; initial teacher training; diploma and higher degree courses in education, in specialist subjects or in education management; plus a variety of short courses and conferences on a wide range of topics. It is quite common to

16

find colleges where the institutional definition of
staff development encompasses only this type of activity,
or places emphasis on the importance of the taught
course.

Items which are categorized sometimes as direct and sometimes as indirect include secondment to industrial or
commercial organizations; research, whether or not this
leads to a qualification; consultancies; exchange to
other educational institutions either at home or abroad;
and planned job rotation, though for practical reasons
this last kind of opportunity is often impossible,
particularly in small colleges and departments carrying
out very specialized work. Finally, there are the items
which are invariably classified as indirect, largely on
the grounds that they can occur independently of a
structured programme. It should, however, be stressed
that the experience of these indirect items are undoubtedly of greater value where they are part of a
planned individual development programme and can be
consolidated by instruction and guidance. Examples
which may be cited here are: service on internal
committees and working parties, or on external examining
boards and course committees; responsibilities for student selection and enrolment, timetabling, and other
aspects of college and departmental organization; preparation of internal reports and memoranda; and production of financial estimates.

That many colleges choose to place emphasis on the
taught course has already been mentioned. Other variations between programmes in both content and method of
approach can be identified. While some make very effective use of their internal resources, others rely almost
exclusively on external provision; while some concentrate on initial training and the improvement of teaching skills, others offer opportunities for the enhancement of a much wider range of skills. Often this reflects broader issues within the FE sector: following
Circular 11/77 attention was turned to initial and post-
experience teacher training; more recently, new course
developments and organizational structures have increased
the demand for training in administration and management;
if the service contracts in the future, then likely
issues will become retraining, redeployment, welfare and
counselling. Indeed, in some colleges moves in this
direction are already apparent.

Perceived benefits
Principals in all of the colleges participating in the

17

study were asked in their initial questionnaire to indicate their perceptions of the benefits accruing from the
introduction of a staff development programme. The many
common elements in their responses are illustrated in
the comments of one respondent which may serve as an
example: 'For the college it provides a more effective
management structure, which in turn will produce a more
professionally competent staff; an improvement in efficiency; improved human relations and communications; and
a greater contribution by staff to the development of
the college because of their involvement, consultation
and participation in decision-making. For the individual it promises an increase in job satisfaction due to
greater competence; an improvement in competence and
other personal qualities; a better understanding of administrative structure and method; and better promotion
prospects'. This last point is naturally being hotly
contested within the colleges and, in certain cases,
being dropped from the aims of the staff development
programme as unrealistic. The argument focussing on
this question is often felt to be fundamental to staff
reactions to a given programme and will be taken up
again later in this chapter.

In addition to the items listed above, six principals
also included the notion of encouraging staff to work
together and to provide one another with mutual support
in developing teaching programmes. Only one made
specific mention of staff development as 'supporting the
policy commitment to research and thus improving our
credibility in submitting proposals to the CNAA'. In a
sample of colleges involved more closely with courses of
advanced further education this kind of comment would
undoubtedly have been of far greater prominence. Again,
only one principal made reference to a frequently forgotten element of staff development: that of 'providing
the necessary refreshment for teachers who have needed a
break after a long period of routine teaching'. As well
as the benefits accruing to teachers, it should also be
noted that many colleges intend their staff development
programme to encompass the development of non-teaching
staff members.

The identification of needs

The observation was made in the previous chapter that
staff development schemes operating within the further
education sector tend to have reached an uncomfortable
compromise between the 'management' and 'democratic'
approaches. Along with the arguments for self-evalua-
tion, self-initiated development, and individually

18

identified priorities, there exists the no less strongly
held view that staff development programmes should cater
primarily for the present and future needs of the institution and must be closely and systematically integrated
within an overall college development plan. Thus the
definitions and statements of aims, which are usually
outlined at the start of each college's policy document,
invariably make some reference to the notion that staff
development schemes are designed to be functional for
both college and individual interests. It is implied
not only that these interests present no problems of
identification, but also that they may be expected to
coincide. The document reproduced as Item 2.1 does
refer to an appeals procedure to which staff have re-
course if an application is refused. This is, however,
a notable exception. As a general rule policy statements make no reference to the potential conflict between the requirements of the individual and the institution, and hence fail to incorporate details of
mechanisms for dealing with such conflict when it arises.

It is implied, moreover, that individual needs also coincide with individual wishes, which means that the voluntary co-operation of staff in any development scheme is
taken for granted. The examples of policy statements
provided here demonstrate that there is never an
explicit reference to any element of compulsion - in
fact it is usually stated quite categorically that participation is on a voluntary basis - and again no details
of mechanisms for dealing with non-cooperation are given.
Staff at all levels will readily admit that an effective
policy has still to be formulated to cater for the
teacher who is performing badly but who, for one reason
or another, will not come forward to take up available
opportunities for improvement.

The approach from the individual member of staff continues to be the essential element in the organization
of staff development, which therefore is less closely
integrated to an overall college plan than policy statements seem to suggest. The underlying philosophy does
not concede that there may be psychological or purely
pragmatic barriers against admitting an inadequacy; and
it is generally the case that no formally established
mechanisms exist to facilitate the identification of
weaknesses as part of a continuous process rather than
an *ad hoc* reaction to specific criticisms.

The tension between the requirements of co-ordination
and those of professionality is a recurrent theme within
the teaching profession, yet any reference to the identi-

fication of needs must immediately encounter it. Unfortunately the very term appraisal has come to be associated in FE with destructive criticism. Senior staff we
talked with often remarked that they could 'see a strong
case for appraisal, but will find it impossible to implement'. Even the management-orientated ACFHE/APTI
report (1973), while recommending the use of an
appraisal procedure, actually suggested a somewhat di-
luted version of those used in industry, on the grounds
that: 'It is by no means certain that such relatively
sophisticated systems are either professionally acceptable, desirable or appropriate in further education'
(p18). What was in fact recommended was 'a formal
system in which every employee is interviewed by his
superior at regular intervals.... To discuss the
teachers' strengths and weaknesses constructively and to
commend or give advice as required' (pp18-19). This
interview technique is commonly used in colleges,
details of how the system will operate being laid down
in the staff development policy document.

A common alternative for identifying needs is by a
questionnaire asking for information on, for instance,
personal details; educational background; specialist
professional work; teaching and administrative experience; courses attended; and immediate and long-term
professional aspirations. Here, as with the interview
method, the emphasis is on the self-identification of
needs by the individual member of staff and on the
voluntary nature of participation in a staff development
programme.

The majority viewpoint among teachers participating in
our study was that staff development policies reflect an
underlying intention - which is never actually stated -
to cater for the ambitious rather than encouraging all
staff to identify and work to overcome any existing weaknesses. It is in private conversation, rather than
public statement, that the likelihood that those who come
forward are not the ones in real need is seen as problematic. As two heads of department in different colleges
noted: 'Our programme seems to offer the opportunity for
good teachers to improve because they are interested in
improving. It does little to identify a need for improvement in individuals'; and 'The fact that the programme is voluntary is an obvious drawback. The very
people who need development do not get it, while the
same group of keen staff members continually avail themselves of the opportunities presented'. Staff at other
grades supported this view from their own experiences.
On the other hand, there were those who believed that

20

the initiative should remain with the individual, the college playing a supporting and facilitating role: 'There seems little point in having staff attend courses they are not interested in. Any approach should be made by the individual. At the same time opportunities should be widely and efficiently publicised by the college'. Teachers who espoused this view often expressed resentment when college demands appeared to have been given priority over individual wishes.

Similarly, staff expressed dissatisfaction when their institution seemed to have adopted so narrow a definition of staff development that a variety of opportunities were effectively closed to them. The most common instance of this situation is that of colleges where resource priority has been given to initial teacher training to the virtual exclusion of all else. In cases such as these it may be argued that the programme fails in that it does not recognize that staff development is a continuous process, with relevance at each stage of a teacher's career. As such, it must recognize both career planning and the needs of individuals unlikely to rise above their current posts. Here, however, the general confusion over the relationship between staff development and promotion enters the debate.

Preparation for promotion

It has already been noted that specific reference in college policy documents to preparing staff for promotion is being dropped by some institutions to be replaced by references to job enrichment. In the absence of a clear definition of the nature and purpose of staff development programmes it is perhaps inevitable that opinions differ markedly as to the effect the current job situation will have on their future. On the one hand, we have found that a significant obstacle to the implementation of initiatives is the view that they are a luxury in times of unemployment and economic cutbacks and that, in any case, staff development schemes will fail without the promise of extrinsic rewards acting as an incentive to participation. The idea that staff development is a temporary experimental exercise peripheral to the main task of the institution is reinforced by this view. There are two fundamental issues here which will have to be clarified at the policy level. Firstly, there is the common understanding that references to preparation for promotion means that promotion will automatically ensue from the take-up of development opportunities. In fact a direct relation of this nature between career advancement and staff development cannot

21

logically work since it immediately raises the question
of establishing criteria for success: for instance, is
quantity of opportunities taken up better or more de-
serving than quality, and how is the relative quality of
different types of activity to be assessed? Colleges
very rarely publish statements of internal promotion
criteria which staff regard as sufficiently specific to
be of any value as an accurate reflection of reality.
Secondly, there is the paradox inherent in the issue of
incentives: having made staff development voluntary on
the assumption that the needs and wishes of individuals
and the demands of the institution invariably coincide,
the notion that decreased promotion prospects will
undermine staff development schemes implies that staff
will volunteer only for instrumental reasons and that
some new kind of bargaining strategy will have to be
found to ensure participation in the future.

There is, however, another view which regards the
present period as one of rationalization rather than
stagnation, in which creativity and imagination are
required to establish new organizational structures and
channels of communication. It is assumed in this case
that interest will increase in a wider concept of staff
development embodied in programmes offering a varied
range of activities, which will enable the teacher not
only to improve his or her existing skills but to
diversify his or her interests to meet new external demands being placed on the colleges. It is, of course,
to be hoped that this view prevails. It will depend on
policy makers tackling the kinds of unresolved problem
outlined in this chapter as the foundation for a rational and responsive style of staff development.

Informal arrangements

Six colleges in the study have no formal policy statement on staff development, largely on the grounds that
any attempt at formalization would result in a decrease
in the inherent flexibility of the programme. In these
colleges it was frequently argued by senior staff
members that formalization was unnecessary since staff
development goes on independently within departments.
Staff below head of department status were, however,
less convinced of the value of this arrangement, often
suggesting that it resulted in *ad hoc* and unco-ordinated
procedures.

The lack of any kind of formal policy statement means
that staff tend to be unaware of the criteria used in
granting applications for staff development activities,

and this is often seen as creating conflict between departments whose staff regard themselves as competing
for limited resources. In order to avoid the accusation
of unfair and arbitrary judgements being made, even
those colleges who reject the notion of an overall
policy are finding that they must publish lists of
selection criteria. One of the six colleges in our investigation has, for example, produced a set of priorities which were drawn up by the staff development
committee, and demonstrate the existence of an implicit
policy with similar assumptions to those stated explicitly in the policy documents of other institutions.
Staff are able to find an account of these guidelines
in the college handbook, but many still felt that in the
absence of stated college or departmental policy the
criteria were insufficiently specific to avoid allega-
tions of bias.

Evaluation of policy and practice

We found little evidence of the existence of formalized
and systematic procedures for evaluating staff development policy and practice. Indeed, in several cases the
policy document and related procedures had not changed
since their initial formulation to take account of new
circumstances or to include improvements and modifica-
tions which had emerged in the light of experience. Only
four colleges reported that policy development was a
standing item on the agenda at either staff development
committee or Academic Board level, while in the remaining
fifteen it was reported that some discussion on staffdevelopment matters did take place from time to time at
both committee and departmental levels. By far the most
common practice in all of the colleges was to carry out
fairly unsystematic evaluations of specific courses,
forms of secondment or other types of activity by using
the reports provided by staff who have recently undertaken development opportunities. It is for instance
quite common for new teachers to be asked to comment on
the design and content of induction courses and to offer
suggestions for improvement. Similarly reports on external courses and conferences may be part of a formal
requirement made by the college for attendance.

Overview

This chapter has sought to describe the content of
college staff development policy documents and to identify
some of their philosophical underpinnings. The design of
such documents is beset with essentially political complications and certainly is not the straightforward task that
it may at first appear. Whatever the difficulties

involved, our evidence would indicate that the production, publication and dissemination of such documents should be regarded as an essential element of any staff development scheme.

Democratically defined and universally understood college objectives must be clearly stated as the framework within which priorities will be set and individual applications judged. A structure which demonstrates consensus is more likely to win support and encourage participation. It does, however, require careful consideration to be made of a number of important issues. Firstly, the roles, functions, responsibilities and limits of power of different grades and individuals need precise definition, if postential conflicts and inconsistencies are to be resolved. It must also be established whether ultimate executive responsibility rests with a department, unit, committee or individual. Secondly, firm decisions are necessary on procedures for identifying needs and for reconciling inst itutional and individual objectives where these fail to coincide. At present, statements in this area are often confused or contradictory; arguments for voluntary, self-initiated development standing alongside those advocating the contentious practice of staff appraisal. It is commonly argued - and not without justification - that staff development programmes cater for the ambitious, and not at all for those who cannot or will not see a need for improvement in their work. Effective programmes must assist not only these two extreme groups but also those who are performing competently and successfully but are unlikely to rise above their current post. Policy documents must make clear the fact that staff development is about job satisfaction at all levels as well as about career-planning and advancement.

A further area of concern is the content and range of the various types of opportunity to be included in the college definition of staff development. Here institutions vary enormously. Our findings suggest that every attempt should be made to offer as wide a range as possible to cater for the great variety of needs that can be identified in any college, always ensuring that the part played by each type of activity within a co-ordinated programme is made apparent. Whatever the approach eventually adopted, those responsible for the formulation of policy must be encouraged to see this not as a once-and-for-all task, but as a continuous process which will enable the college to respond quickly and effectively to meet changes occuring in the broader FE system.

Item 2.1

POLICY FOR STAFF DEVELOPMENT

1.   Staff Development and College Academic Policy

1.1 Academic Goals

The primary task of the College is to achieve its
stated academic goals; namely, in its role as a
Community College, to offer within the scope of its
own organisation a comprehensive provision of
further and higher education, based on principles
that deny no student access to qualifications or
higher education, and that relate to the needs of an
urban, industrial, multi-cultural society.

1.2 Staff Development Policy

1.2.1   The staff development policy will be to
further the achievement of these academic
goals:

i) by identifying the College's training
needs and the appropriate forms of staff
development;

ii) by initiating, as required, appropriate
action to meet such needs;

and   iii) by providing opportunities for the staff
of the College to improve their qualifications, expertise and general contribution
to the work of the College.

1.2.2   Since the College's budget includes funds designated for staff development for full-time
established members of staff, the normal
College staff development policy will be to
support full-time staff members. Nevertheless the Staff Development Sub-Committee re-
cognises its responsibilities for part-time
staff where no assistance is available from
any other source and under those circumstances
will support part-time members of staff using
the same criteria as those for full-time
members.

In order to calculate the amount of financial
assistance for staff development for non-
teaching staff, the College should determine
a sum of money for the assistance of non-
teaching staff which would a) represent a
nominal ceiling and b) be based on the actual

25

costs of training. The sum would be an equivalent proportion of the non-teaching staff costs to that proportion of the teaching salaries which is devoted to staff development for teaching staff. It would include allowances for fees and expenses, whether paid or waived, plus the notional costs of replacement for any time-off allowed.

The Staff Development Sub-Committee would not normally give back allowance to any member of staff unless a special case could be made.

1.3 Policy Implementation

1.3.1 Staff Development Sub-Committee

The Staff Development Sub-Committee shall be responsible for making recommendations relating to the implementation and monitoring of the College's staff development policy. It shall receive applications for leave-of-absence and financial assistance and make recommendations about such applications to the Staffing Committee. It shall store and disseminate information about opportunities and courses for staff development through the College Library Services and advise members of staff as appropriate.

It shall initiate College staff development programmes and liaise with the regional services for in-service training.

It shall advise Schools and Faculties from time to time about current staff development policies.

1.3.2 Role of the Schools

Each School shall maintain its own Staff Development Committee which shall consider the implementation of its Staff Development Policy and make recommendations to the College's Staff Development Sub-Committee through the Head of School.

It shall also be responsible for determining which members of the School shall attend courses and for the disbursement of funds for attendance on short courses and conferences.

26

1.3.3 Role of the Faculties

Each Faculty shall have specific responsibility for staff development in its area of "subject" expertise and provide a source of professional advice for staff development within that area. It shall review the qualifications of members of the Faculty, noting areas where development is needed, and shall make recommendations, either through the School or directly to the Staff Development Sub-Committee, as to the appropriate action to be taken.

2. Underlying Principles

2.1 All staff shall have similar opportunities to seek College aid for staff development but the criteria for allocating College resources shall be related to the achievement of the College's academic goals (as set out in 1.1 above).

2.2 Three main criteria will be used in determining priorities for staff development. Applications for College assistance will be considered by the Staff Development Sub-Committee according to the following order of priorities:

a) firstly, for requests to follow specific programmes, which are perceived to be of direct benefit to the College;

b) secondly, for requests to follow programmes less specifically related to the current work of a given member of staff, but that will increase the flexibility of members of staff in meeting identified needs of the College or the region, in the first instance, or other socially or educationally desirable goals in a wider context;

and c) thirdly, requests to follow programmes for the personal benefit of the individual.

2.3 In applying these criteria, the Staff Development Sub-Committee shall have regard to the immediate needs of the College for that person's services, but shall also endeavour to maintain the principle of opportunity as described in 2.1 above so as to ensure that no individual is disadvantaged over time.

2.4 The underlying principles and the order of priorities as described above apply equally to non-teaching staff as well as to academic staff. It is, however,

27

recognized that the implementation of these principles may have to be somewhat different, in order to ensure consistency with the conditions of service under which people are employed and any relevant national agreements concerning such conditions of service.

2.5 In addition to considering applications from members of staff, the Staff Development Sub-Committee reserve the right to initiate a staff development proposal and as a response to changes, or intended changes, in College policy or patterns of work to allocate resource to meet the needs of retraining staff as part of a College relocation policy.

2.6 Whenever support is related to the relocation or retraining of staff the entire costs will normally be met by the College.

2.7 Whenever other sources of financial assistance are available, the members of staff will be required to seek support in the first instance.

3. Forms of Staff Development

3.1 Full-time, established members of staff will be given support to follow courses, whether these be provided by the College as part of its curriculum or be external agencies, in the following ways:

a) Full-time secondment.

b) Release from some part of normal terms of employment to follow a course.

c) Assistance with the costs of attending such courses, eg. fees, travel expenses, subsistance.

d) Re-arrangement of normal terms of employment to facilitate attendance on a course.

3.2 Criteria for full-time secondments

3.2.1 The criteria for full-time secondments shall first be related to the general Staff Development policy as agreed.

3.2.2 That the nature of the work which the applicant shall normally be expected to undertake on his/her return shall be determined before approval for secondment may be given.

3.2.3 That such work will be negotiated by the Staff Development Sub-Committee with the Heads of School involved.

3.2.4 That the advice of the Faculties in determining such work will be sought by the Staff Development Sub-Committee.

3.2.5 a) In particular, the College's training and re-training needs will be used to determine priorities, and the re-training of staff for redeployment will be given prior consideration.

b) The advice of the appropriate relocation committee will be sought in determining such redeployment and re-training needs.

3.3 Part-time members of staff will normally only receive financial assistance in support of their staff development neees as in 3.1(c).

3.4 In addition, the College intends to extend and develop its own in-service staff development programme. The College will endeavour to provide a programme with four main emphases:

a) Induction courses - all new members of staff will be required to attend some form of induction course.

b) Courses to meet statutory requirements - these will relate to legal requirements, eg. health and safety.

c) Courses to improve staff effectiveness in carrying out the terms of their appointment, eg. in teacher training, in management skills, in extending technical skills, or in increasing their flexibility.

d) Courses in curriculum development and planning for academic staff and in work planning and development for other members of staff.

3.5 Whenever full-time permanent members of College attend College courses as part of staff development programmes, their fees shall be waived.

3.6 In determining the nature of the support to be given, the Staff Development Sub-Committee shall determine whether the costs shall be met in full or in part.

4. Frames of Reference

Having agreed on the members of staff who shall be supported, the nature of the courses required and the ways in which the needs of individual members of staff are to be met, the Staff Development Sub-Committee shall follow the guide lines as described below:

a) the first frame of reference will be to the College provision to determine whether a suitable course is available or whether the College has the appropriate resources or expertise to mount such a course on a cost-effective basis;

b) the second frame of reference will be to the local and regional provision to determine whether suitable courses are available;

c) the third frame of reference will be to determine whether these needs can be met on a part-time basis;

d) the final frame of reference will be to agree to full-time secondment. (Normally, the equivalent of nine full-time members of the academic staff shall be allowed to attend full-time courses in each term and the College is actively exploring whether similar opportunities can be offered to other full-time members of the staff.)

5. Constitution and Composition of Staff Development Sub-Committee

5.1 Constitution

The Staff Development Sub-Committee shall be a committee of the College Staff Committee, but its membership shall not be restricted to members of the Committee. It shall be responsible, through the Director of Academic Planning, to the Staffing Committee for decisions on the allocation of College resources to staff development and for monitoring the process of staff development throughout the College and its constituent Schools.

5.2 Composition

Its membership shall consist of The Principal, or nominee, Chief Administrative Officer, or nominee, Vice-Principal - Director of Academic Planning, 5 Heads of Schools, 5 Heads of Faculties, 9 elected members of academic staff, 2 representatives of the Students' Union and 3 elected members of the non-teaching staff (1 representative each from the administrative, technical and manual staff).

6. Methods of application

6.1 Long Courses

6.1.1 These shall normally refer to courses or periods of absence of one term or more which may either lead to some formal academic qualification or allow the member of staff to gain particular experience as approved by the Staff Development Sub-Committee.

6.1.2 Members of staff shall make application for assistance on the officially approved forms on agreed dates. The application shall be counter-signed by the members of staff's designated superior, eg. Head of Schools, Executive Head of Faculty or Staffing Officer.

6.2 Short Courses and Conferences

6.2.1 These shall normally refer to conferences or courses not exceeding fourteen days in length.

6.2.2 Members of staff shall apply directly to their designated superiors.

6.3 Other forms

Members of staff seeking assistance in any other form shall first seek advice of the Director of Academic Planning.

6.4 Refused Applications

6.4.1 Where the designated superior refuses the application, or to countersign it, the member of staff may apply directly to the Staff Development Sub-Committee through the Director of Academic Planning.

6.4.2 Whenever the Staff Development Sub-Committee turns down an application, the members of staff may appeal to the Staffing Committee.

Item 2.2

STAFF DEVELOPMENT : A STATEMENT OF COLLEGE POLICY

Definition

"A systematic process by which an individual's knowledge, skills and personal qualities can be broadened, deepened and enlarged to the benefit of the individual, the department in which he operates and the organisation that employs him".

The Need

Staff development will take place within a college even in the absence of any formal staff development policy. In such circumstances development will take place haphazardly and affect only those staff who, in their own initiative, wish to enhance their own level and range of performance. The under-developed qualities of other members of staff, who are perhaps less ambitious or more diffident, are likely to remain under-developed.

Such a college is unlikely to be working at maximum efficiency, for it will not be possible to realise the full potential of the staff if they are not encouraged to develop this potential and given the opportunity to do so. There will tend to be a general lack of experimentation, innovation, and of impetus and this will be reflected in the general development of the college and, in consequence, its service to industry and its students.

The Aims

A planned staff development policy is therefore necessary and has advantages both for the college and for all staff. This document sets out the staff development policy of the College as approved by the college Academic Board at its meeting on the 9th November, 1971, (minute 71/25 refers) and subsequently amended. The aims of the policy which apply equally to the academic and non-academic staff may be stated as follows:

For the College

A more effective management structure which will provide:

(1) A more professionally competent staff.
(2) An improvement in efficiency.
(3) Improved human relations and communications.
(4) A greater contribution by staff to the development of the college, because of their involvement, consultation and participation in decision-making.

32

For the Staff

(1) An increase in job satisfaction due to greater competence.
(2) An improvement in confidence and other personal qualifites.
(3) A better understanding of administrative structure and method.
(4) Better promotion prospects due to increased competence and enhanced personal qualities.

The Nature of the Exercise

Indirect Factors in Staff Development

Opportunities for staff development will occur independently of any structured development programme, for example, the election of staff to various internal college committees and working parties, the invitation to specialist staff to participate from time to time in educational activities external to the college, such as examinerships, service on Regional Examining Boards, inter-college exercises in course and curriculum development, and so on. Such activities should be encouraged.

The Direct Factors

Although there will be many opportunities for staff development on a group basis (for example, internal and external staff courses), there will also be a need to discuss with staff their own development requirements, and in general each member of staff will require his/her individual development programme.

Not all staff will wish to participate in a staff development programme. It may be for example that a member of staff finds that his present job gives him full satisfaction, is financially independent, and has no wish to seek further promotion. Another member of staff may feel himself to be fully extended at his present level. The staff development programme must be able to adapt to such situations, and although the programme must reflect the development policy of the college as a whole, it will ultimately be a matter for the personal agreement of staff concerned, in consultation with the Department Head.

A Staff Development Policy for the Academic Staff

Staff development courses are already provided by the Further Education Staff College for senior staff, and are concerned mainly with policy and management at departmental and college level, and with major policy

33

changes affecting further education. At a lower level, summer schools and other courses are organised by the D.E.S. and by Regional Councils. The college policy includes the planned support of such courses, and will seek to reinforce them by staff seminars in which all staff have the opportunity to discuss the effects of major changes in educational policy on the future of the college. Course reports by those attending could well form the basis for such seminars and could be presented as papers by the course-goers themselves.

It is at the lower level, perhaps, that an internal staff development policy can be most effective in improving the efficiency of the individual, and hence, the college. There are, for instance, no courses within the further education system which provide training in the basic routine of administration, and practically none outside the training colleges which encourage experimentation in new teaching methods.

An examination of the skills and qualities required of the teaching staff for the efficient functioning of the college has identified the following areas as relevant to a staff development programme.

(1) Education.
(2) Administration.
(3) Personal development.

The following specific development activities have been recommended for each of these areas.

Education

Professional Teacher Status

The College of Education (Further) now provide a variety of courses leading to professional teacher status (including in-service sandwich courses). The staff development programme includes the planned support of such courses.

Subject Knowledge

(1) Updating of specialist knowledge.
(2) Extension of specialisation into other subject areas.
(3) Subject relevance and application.

The staff development policy includes staff sponsorship for specialist subject courses on a planned basis.

Internally, arrangements can be made within and between departments by which staff can assist more experienced colleagues with advanced courses in their own specialisms, and with courses in other subject areas.

The teacher's knowledge of the relevance and application of his subject to modern technology may be updated by his periodic release to industry, or by a requirement that he should periodically attend conferences and trade exhibitions, and these activities form a planned part of the staff development programme.

Experimentation in New Teaching Methods

Planned opportunities can be provided for staff to experiment and gain experience in the selection and use of a wide range of teaching techniques (team teaching, small group tutorials, projects, etc.).

It is the responsibility of college departments to provide such opportunities by organizing discussion, forming working groups and encouraging experimentation. In broader areas of interest which concern the college as a whole the initiative might well come in the first instance from the Staff Development Panel, in the organisation of lectures and staff seminars on a college basis.

Experimentation should also be encouraged in new methods of assessment. While traditional examinations remain, however, it should be the policy, within departments, to give teachers experience in this field so that they gain confidence in setting questions of the right content and standard, and which satisfy the course and the syllabus objectives.

Administration

Staff, particularly as they rise in seniority, are likely to find that their duties include delegated administrative responsibilities in addition to their teaching. The staff development programme must therefore provide for basic training in administration so that the college may function smoothly, and staff may have confidence in their ability to undertake such responsibilities when the need arises.

The administrative areas in which staff are most likely to become involved are:

Organizations; finance; communications; records and office procedure.

Within these areas some of the responsibilities will be those of organization and delegation rather than of personal execution, and it must be remembered that the teacher's primary function is to teach. The senior posts in the profession are predominantly administrative, however, many senior staff will be eager to gain admini-

35

strative experience in preparation for promotion. Such experience may include:

Organization

1) Responsibility for class timetables.
Responsibility for staff timetables.
Responsibility for room timetables.

    Possibly as an 'umbrella' responsibility for two or more staff working together.

2) Responsibility for student selection procedures.
3) Responsibility for enrolment arrangements.
4) Responsibility for examination arrangements and timetables.
5) Responsibility for short course organization and publicity.
6) Responsibility for visual aids.
7) Responsibility for laboratory/workshop/studio.

At departmental level, the staff development policy can provide staff experience in the above areas by arranging for a system of understudies.

In addition it is possible for certain duties other than those which are highly critical (such as timetabling) to be rotated between staff from time to time (say, on a three-yearly basis).

Such an arrangement, in which successive members of staff might wish to leave behind them some positive evidence of their period of responsibility, might well stimulate the more vigorous development and use of laboratories, etc.

Finance

At teacher level, involvement will be limited to the following areas:

1) Production of sub-estimates.
2) Purchasing procedures and use of order-books.
3) Maintenance of financial and stock records.
4) Stock check procedures.

Any understudy/rota system should include the provision of experience in these areas.

Communications, Records and Office Procedure

At a more senior level the acceptance of administrative responsibility includes a greater involvement in formal communications, and the need to establish efficient office procedures. In detail this includes:

1) Drafting of internal memoranda and instructions.

2) Dealing with external correspondence.
3) Preparation of reports and minutes.
4) Routine documentation, eg. completion of D.E.S.
   course approval forms, etc.
5) Establishing an efficient information storage/re-
   trieval system (filing, cross-referencing, etc.).
6) Dictation to a stenographer/use of dictaphone.

It is possible to provide formal instruction for senior
staff, in some of these areas, via courses arranged by
the Management and Business Studies Department. For the
remaining areas it will rest with the Head of Department
to provide the necessary experience and training by
delegation, under the supervision of himself or his
deputy (completion of forms 95 F.E., for example).

Personal Development

The development of personal qualities such as confidence,
initiative, leadership, etc, will be largely a question
of providing a suitable environment for the exercise
and growth of these qualities. Many of the delegated
responsibilities already discussed will also provide
such an environment. Others might include:

1) Service on departmental and college committees.
2) Experience as an officer of such committees.
3) Leader of discussion group/working party/development
   project, etc.

Members of staff should from time to time be provided
with, or at least offered, opportunities for the
exercise and development of personal qualities.

Implementation of Staff Development Policy

The Staff Development Panel

Responsibility for implementing and updating staff de-
velopment policy has been delegated by the Academic
Board to the Staff Development Panel. Membership of
this Panel comprises representatives from each of the
following departments: Catering, Fashion and Health,
Construction Industries, Electrical Engineering and
Science, General Education, Management and Business
Studies and Mechanical Engineering together with the
Senior Administrative Officer, who is the Training
Officer for non-academic staff. The Vice Principal and
the Professional Tutor act, respectively, as Chairman
and Secretary to the Panel.

Staff development must be tailored to the needs of the
individual and must bring together college policy, the
opportunities for development which are available within

the college at any given time, the previous experience of the member of staff, and his or her own wishes and ambitions.

A confidential staff development record is therefore maintained for each member of staff, listing qualifications and experience on appointment, and indicating the various areas (discussed above) under which development might take place. The staff development record for each member of staff will normally be reviewed once each year by the Principal/Vice Principal and the Head of Department, together with the member of staff concerned and the development programme for the following year agreed. The record will be updated after each development exercise has been completed. Each member of staff has access to his staff development record at any time.

Those parts of the development policy which deal with the release of staff from teaching duties for various purposes require policy decisions at Governing Body/ Local Authority level.

Staff Relations

In the interest of good staff relations it is important that the purpose, nature and method of implementation of the staff development policy should be clearly understood by the staff. All new staff should be informed of the policy at their appointment interview, and given a copy of this policy document on appointment.

Counselling

The first year of appointment, for new staff, will be needed as a settling in period. It is unlikely that such staff will be involved in the staff development programme at this stage apart from the induction programme for new staff. It is useful if experienced members of staff act as counsellors to new staff during their first year of service, and all new appointees to the college should be assigned to a counsellor by their Head of Department.

The Professional Tutor is responsible for the induction programme, which includes the counselling of new staff during their probationary year. His duties also include the coordination of both internal and external teacher training programmes and he is available to advise all staff on such matters as retraining and further professional training.

CHAPTER 3

Decision-making structures

For some years now there has been increasing pressure
placed on colleges from both internal and external
sources to move towards a more organic model. By 1970
the general movement towards the democratization of institutions evident throughout society had produced for
further education a government response in the form of
DES Circular 7/70. A recent commentary on this document
has noted: 'One effect of the breakthrough which 7/70 re-
presented was to highlight just how minimal had been the
rights of teaching staff to participate in the decision-
making processes in the colleges in which they worked.
However, by establishing that college staff were entitled
to representation on Governing Bodies and that colleges
should have Academic Boards, it was at least acknowledged
that teachers had a part to play both in the government
of the colleges and in the development of their academic
work...'(Thomas and Levine, 1979, p10). By 1976 NATFHE
Conference was pressing for a revision of Circular 7/70
which would include an assurance that all college boards
and committees would function as executive rather than
simply as consultative bodies.

In common with other organizations, further education
institutions demonstrate the phenomenon that as the locus
of power becomes more diffuse it becomes correspondingly
more difficult to determine who makes a given decision,
when and how. This chapter discusses the formal structures which have been established within colleges to
facilitate decision-making specifically in the area of
staff development, and describes staff's own views of the
efficacy of the procedures adopted in their particular
institution.

The staff development committee

A general pattern exists for colleges to have a staff

development committee (with slight variations in name), which is a subcommittee of and is responsible to the Academic Board as the final internal decision-making body. Fifteen of our nineteen colleges had such a committee. The usual composition of a staff development committee is as follows: the vice-principal (who acts as chairperson), all heads of department, the professional tutor and staff development officer(s) where these exist, elected representatives from each department, plus the power to co-opt 'other members with special interest in staff development'. Resources and administration staff are included in a small number of cases and a variety of individuals may be invited to specific meetings where they have a particular interest or expertise in items on the agenda. There are, of course, variations in this pattern: for example, heads of department may be members only if elected as their departmental representatives; there is sometimes a NATFHE representative (though only in three of the colleges in our sample); in one college there is a student representative nominated by the students' union; and, perhaps most strikingly, the staff development committee of another college always includes a teacher of personnel management. While membership is most commonly by free election, four colleges stipulate that members drawn from the teaching staff are appointed directly by the Academic Board. Committee members normally serve for three years with one member retiring each year. In all but one college operating an election system all members are eligible for re-election.

All the colleges participating in our investigation supplied us with the terms of reference of all internal committees with some responsibility in the area of staff development. The terms of reference of specifically designated staff development committees showed few variations at the general level. Members are appointed to monitor the implementation of existing policy, to ensure the equitable access of all staff to development opportunities and resources, to identify and keep under review staff training and development needs, to advise the Academic Board on the resource implications of the staff development policy, to recommend policy changes to the Academic Board, and generally to promote staff development within the college. Indeed, in certain colleges the stated terms of reference go into no further detail.

Perhaps the main point to emerge from these statements is the fact that staff development committees are essentially advisory rather than executive. Certainly Academic Boards tend to retain control over policy and priorities, and to make the final decision on these

matters after receiving recommdnations from the staff
development committee. The terms of reference reproduced as Item 3.1 give some indication of the specific
areas of policy in which committee members may be invited to present their recommendations. This particular
example in fact refers to a committee currently operating
in a large institution (250 full-time staff), and demonstrates how it can also be required to act as the centre
of a communications network receiving and filtering information to be passed on to the Academic Board.

In six of the colleges in our study the committee was
also responsible for drawing up the college's staff development policy, though again the final decision on
content rests with the Academic Board. When it comes to
the implementation of policy, committees may find themselves able to act in a more executive capacity. On the
question of approving applications for secondment and
release, for example, in most colleges the committee is
empowered to make recommendations which must then be
forwarded for approval to the Academic Board. In other
colleges the committee can itself grant formal approval
for attendance at short courses and, in two colleges, at
long courses including those of initial teacher training.

In four colleges the types of activity required of committee members are given explicit attention in the terms
of reference. In the document reproduced as Item 3.2
for example, it is made clear that members are to take
an active role in the actual provision of development
opportunities for their colleagues. In another college
members of the committee are charged with the responsibility for acting as tutors and mentors to newly appointed teachers - a scheme that is presently under discussion in other colleges we visited. The committee may
also be expected to 'store and disseminate information
about opportunities and courses for staff development
through the college library services and advise members
of staff as appropriate'. Although by no means always
so explicitly stated, it is in fact fairly common for
staff development committee members to be required to
perform duties of this kind - particuarly in colleges
where no professional tutor appointment has been made.

Additional committees

In addition to the college staff development committee,
there are a number of other formally constituted bodies
within each institution which directly or indirectly
take part in staff development decision-making from the
point of view of their particular areas of interest. The

TERMS OF REFERENCE AGREED BY THE ACADEMIC BOARD FOR THE
STAFF DEVELOPMENT COMMITTEE

That a standing Committee of the Academic Board be established, called the Staff Development Committee, with the following terms of reference:-

(i)   To review the whole area of activity in the College relevant to the term "Staff Development".

(ii)   To recommend policy to the Academic Board in each main area of topics concerning staff development.

(iii) In particular, to recommend policy and procedures in each of the following areas:-
       (a) Manpower planning
       (b) Staff records
       (c) Staff training; re-training; re-deployment
       (d) Induction; Staff Handbook
       (e) Criteria for Secondment and Study Leave (including short courses)
       (f) Liaison with commerce and industry in respect of (1) supernumerary secondment and (2) College Project Service
       (g) Liaison with schools and other public services as in (f) above
       (h) Staff appraisal in respect of performance and potential
       (i) Criteria for promotion
       (j) Implementation of employment legislation in the College

(iv)   To recommend priorities for implementation and any vote of resources in a staff development strategy.

(v)   To liaise closely with those concerned with the College development plan in order to match deliberations with the declared development intentions of the College.

(vi)   To have power to appoint Working Parties in any specialist area, where this is thought by the Committee to be desirable, the members of which need not be members of the Staff Development Committee.

(vii) To be enabled to canvass the staff at large about important areas of staff development policy and to co-opt to appointed Working Parties any member of staff who has shown a particular interest in a subject.

(viii) To be responsible for the timetable of Working

Party reports and to receive, in the first instance, all such reports and to review their placement in the overall staff development strategy.

(ix)   To be responsible for bringing these Working Party reports and the views of the Staff Development Committee to the Academic Board in the form of a full report on each chosen topic area.

(x)   To liaise with the Staff Development Committees established in the departments, with a view to learning the particular interests of each department.

Item 3.2

The Staff Development Committee

This is a sub-committee of the Academic Board and as such exists to advice the Board on matters relating to staff training and development.

The main functions of the Committee are:-

1. to give advice to staff on those courses which may be of use to them
2. to make recommendations to the Academic Board for financial support to staff on long courses
3. to run a basic training course for staff without teaching qualifications
4. to run an induction programme for newly appointed staff
5. to provide tutorial support for staff attending the in-service Certificate in Education Course
6. to run a series of lectures and discussion on educational topics
7. to organize training periods on educational topics and teaching techniques for part-time staff
8. to provide induction courses for non-teaching staff and to keep them informed of general College development
9. oversight of the central audio-visual aids provision
10.support for students on teaching practice from other colleges.

committee of heads of department was most commonly mentioned by principals in this context, together with the committee responsible for the administration and development of library and technological resources, and a variety of committees responsible for the development of specific courses whose remit often includes the identification of consequent staff training needs. In three of the larger colleges each department also has its own departmental staff development committee which, within the limits of the overall policy statement, has a reasonable degree of autonomy in deciding, for example, on areas of priority. In two colleges the principals mentioned the indirect influence exerted by their principal's advisory committees, whose remit is to provide advice on all aspects of the work undertaken by the college. Only one college operates a committee consisting solely of the vice-principal and staff development officers, which is 'primarily concerned with professional or academic matters rather than with the broader issues of policy'. This committee may, for example, meet to consider a specific aspect of teaching the City and Guilds 730 course.

Alternative structures

This, then, is the overall pattern of committee input into staff development decision-making. There are, however, four exceptions of colleges where no staff development committee exists. The first is a relatively small college which has only recently begun to consider staff development matters within a formal framework. The principal reports that, instead of there being one committee with a general remit in this area, there are five separate boards in addition to the heads of departments' committee who are responsible for advising the Academic Board on particular areas of staff development need. However, it must be said that primary responsibility for decisions on staff development matters rests with the principal, vice-principal and heads of department. Indeed the principal commented at interview that 'there is no need for staff to be involved'. Teachers themselves were divided on the question of how far they were able to contribute to the decision-making process, though by a slight majority the feeling was that they were able to make informal contributions at departmental level but that their views were usually ignored in relation to overall college policy: 'We have the opportunity to present our views about departmental matters and course design but not about the larger policy issues'; 'We are consulted, but there is a difference between consultation and participation'.

The second college has a much longer history of interest
in staff development and made one of the first appointments in the country of a full-time professional tutor.
After modifying the policy document drawn up by the
tutor, the existing staff development committee was
disbanded and has not been replaced. The heads of departments' committee and the tutor himself now report
directly to the Academic Board on all staff development
matters. In addition the college has a research committee which discusses those aspects of staff development
that are specifically related to its research brief.
Again staff were divided over whether they had the opportunity to participate in the decision-making process, but
in fairness it must be stated that many did not in fact
want such an opportunity. A typical comment was: 'In
practice I leave this to my colleagues, but my voice
would be heard should I choose to involve myself'.

The principal of the third college stated that heads of
department and the Academic Board are the primary decision-making bodies on questions relating to staff development. In this college it would in fact be true to
say that the heads represent a particularly powerful
force and certainly have no intention of passing any of
the responsibility for the development of their departmental staff to any other section or individual.

The fourth college has a research and secondment sub-
committee of the Academic Board. Its title does not,
however, indicate that it has, as a matter of policy,
attached highest priority to in-service teacher training
and retraining. Individual members of staff apply to
their own departmental board of studies for release or
secondment, and if these applications are approved they
go to the research and secondment committee and to the
Academic Board for final approval. Thus, although the
existing structure is almost the equivalent of the more
usual type of staff development committee, it was generally seen as having an inherent disadvantage in that
staff development activities are never originated by the
committee, but by departmental boards which were regarded
as not having an overview of the needs of the college as
a whole. Departments in this college do in fact have
their own budget for short courses and conferences which
may be disbursed at the discretion of the head.

Staff participation

Heads of department in all but one of the colleges in our
sample were almost unanimous in their agreement that they
were fully consulted on all aspects of their college's
staff development policy. In fact, in some cases heads

felt that they had more power in this area than the staff
development committee, particularly since they play a
central role in approving applications from their departmental staff wanting to take up development opportunities.
In six of the colleges in the sample heads of department
are required to submit an annual report to the staff development committee outlining their departmental programmes of staff development for the coming year and
commenting on current and future priorities. Staff often
informed us that it was 'left to the discretion of HODs
whether decisions reached at the level of the staff development committee are actually implemented'. All those
with major responsibility for staff development within
their respective colleges stressed the importance of
gaining the support of heads to the success of any scheme.
Professional tutors were particularly aware of the potential problem of their 'treading on the toes' of heads
and recognized the fact that their respective roles in
this area must be carefully delineated.

In only one college are heads of department deliberately
excluded from the staff development committee whose
chairman, the vice-principal, argued that he 'did not
want them laying down the law and precluding the active
involvement of junior members of staff'. In consequence
heads are fairly hostile to the committee and resent the
position whereby policy is 'dictated' to their department.
The comment made by one head of department in this
college illustrates the situation that has been created:
'I am afraid that in my opinion staff development as it
presently stands in this college is for the "laugh and
tear up file". Within my department I operate as best I
can with practically zero support and resources. What
is required is a radical change of direction towards the
departments themselves. Staff development programmes
should be decentralized'.

This question of decentralization towards departments in
fact arose on several occasions during interviews with
departmental heads. They frequently pointed to initiatives which had emerged not from the committee but from
enthusiasm generated within individual departments. For
example, heads in one college pointed to the fact that
the college staff development committee had played no
part in introducing a new scheme to enable staff to return to industry. It is not, however, always the case
that heads themselves wish to take on the sole responsibility for staff development matters within their respective departments. While it is true that the majority
are loathe to give up their responsibilities in this
area, a small number do see this aspect of their work as

Item 4.1

SELF-EVALUATION QUESTIONNAIRE FOR TEACHING STAFF

PRE-LESSON

1. Are you using an up-to-date syllabus?
2. Have you broken down the syllabus into a scheme of work?
3. Did you collaborate with others in drawing up the scheme of work?
4. Do you know the capabilities of your students?
5. Is your preparation technically accurate?
6. Are your objectives clear?
7. Will you be ascertaining whether or not the objectives have been achieved?

DURING LESSON

1. Have you introduced the lesson effectively?
2. Do the students know what they are doing and why?
3. Are you trying to motivate your students?
4. Are you enthusiastic in your approach?
5. Are you using an appropriate teaching strategy?
6. Have you <u>actively involved</u> the students in the lesson?
7. Are you using effective question and answer techniques?
8. Are you making adequate use of A.V.A.?
9. Have you arranged the room in a suitable manner?
10. Have you tried to evaluate if the objectives have been achieved?
11. Have you rounded off the lesson, re-inforcing the main points?

SOME INDICATIONS OF INEFFECTIVE TEACHING

1. You have no clear scheme of work.
2. You have no objectives for the lesson.
3. You have no lesson plan.
4. You have given out information oblivious of what the students are doing.
5. You have not actively involved the students in the lesson eg. they are only listening or copying.
6. You have given long dictated notes.
7. Your supporting material was inadequate or poorly prepared.
8. Your students were obviously bored, asleep, or misbehaving.

Item 4.2

CONFIDENTIAL

Details of Staff to be used in support of an application for promotion.

The promotion applied for -
  (a) School of:
  (b) Area of work (If applicable):

(1) NAME   Age

    School of:
    Address:

(2) QUALIFICATIONS

    Academic qualifications with classification and dates:
    Professional qualifications with classification and dates:
    Courses of Study:
    Research and/or Publications:

(3) EXPERIENCE

    (i) Length and variety of experience prior to joining the College Staff:

    (ii) Length and variety of experience within the College:
        a) Teaching experience -

           Subjects taught:

           Grade/Courses:

           Administrative responsibility for Courses:

           Course Development:

           Curriculum Development:

        b) A resume of applicant's present job -

        c) College contribution outside teaching commitments -

(4) Any other relevant information and interests:-

(5) Personal statement by the Applicant (reasons for
    making application):-

---

(6) Reference provided by the Head of School concerned,
    making particular reference to:-

    Standard of work maintained

    Timelines in meeting job objectives

    Initiative

    Adaptability

    Relationships with Staff/Students

    Personal Qualities

Date......... Signed.................(Applicant)

                Signed.................(Head of School)

To be forwarded to the Director by the Applicant.

---

made explicit to teachers the purpose of such a visit. The overwhelming majority of heads of department referred to indirect methods when asked to describe how they identified a teacher's strengths and weaknesses. They most frequently mentioned reference to students' examination results. It was also widely reported that reports from employers, parents, section leaders, HMI, Advisers and students themselves could help in building up a picture of a teacher and his or her performance. In addition it was maintained that further information on the teacher could be gleaned by examining blackboard work after classes, scrutinizing equipment and material orders and noting staff applications for courses and conferences.

Heads considered that senior teachers were generally easier to assess as, in their opinion, administrative proficiency was less difficult to evaluate. There was also likely to be more extensive informal and formal contact between the head and such staff. Several heads referred to the fact that they held regular meetings with section leaders and they were more likely to be members of committees and working parties. Overall, however, heads' reports of their methods for monitoring performance indicated that there was considerable variation in the amount of contact between a head of department and his or her staff - even within the same college. Departmental size and split-site teaching in particular were seen as severely restricting in this context.

It should be stressed that it was not common practice these twelve colleges for heads to discuss their assessments with the teacher concerned. Only when teachers applied for promotion or were perceived to have problems was a head likely to raise the question of their performance. Few heads of department reported that they would point out to staff that their work was unsatisfactory. Most commonly it appeared that this matter would be approached obliquely; the teacher concerned would be encouraged to apply for a course, especially in initial teacher training, if this had not been previously undertaken.

Formal procedures

In the other seven colleges formal procedures had been instituted to assess staff needs. Although all schemes had elements of the ACFHE/APTI appraisal model - even those which had been established prior to the Report - none conformed entirely to the recommended approach. The procedures employed are examined below in the context of the ACFHE/APTI recommendations.

Although staff are provided with job specifications in
four of the colleges they were discussed as a matter of
course at the interview in only one college; even here
they are to be replaced in favour of a 'checklist'. The
job specifications were attached to a position and not
to an individual incumbent, and did not therefore reflect differences regarding specific responsibilities
undertaken. They did, however, exhibit a number of
variations in style and emphasis, as illustrated in
Item 4.3. The two examples given here were in fact
drawn up in colleges of similar size and organizational
structure.

Interviews are held annually or, in one case, on an
eighteen-month recurrent basis, and in all seven colleges
participation is voluntary. While the interview is regarded as an important part of staff development, only
in one instance is it considered to be fundamental.

In four of the colleges staff are interviewed by their
head of department - though in one, where policy is being
revised, it is proposed that in the future staff should
have the option of having either the head of department
or another colleague present. In the words of the chairman of the staff development committee this modification
has been suggested because there is some feeling that 'a
head of department may not be the most appropriate
person to administer the scheme'. Support for this revision also came from those heads who envisaged that it
might reduce the burden which interviewing placed on
them. In all four colleges heads of departments' commitment to interviewing and their conviction regarding its
worth varied considerably. Clearly some felt that the
interviews were superfluous as they were already
thoroughly familiar with the performance and development
requirements of their staff. In the three remaining
colleges interviews are conducted by the vice-principal;
the vice-principal and principal; and the principal respectively. In the college where the vice-principal interviews staff it was reported that his involvement
arose because of staff opposition to heads of department
performing this duty. Here an education lecturer, an
LII, who is regarded as a professional tutor, may also
be present at the discussions. Where both the vice-
principal and principal conduct interviews the former
sees junior staff while senior staff are seen by the
latter. In the third case the principal instituted interviews with staff when he first took up office over
ten years ago. He never delegates this responsibility

Item 4.3

College A. SECTION LEADER

6.1 General

To be responsible to his/her Head of Department for:

(a) A particular area of work in the Department and possibly across the College.
(b) A number of full-time and part-time staff.
(c) A number of full-time and part-time students.

6.2 Duties

(a) Selection of syllabi of work, including suggestion for introduction of new courses.
(b) Supervision of the preparation of Schemes of Work and assistance in the organization of examinations.
(c) General Supervision of Staff, teaching methods and standards in the Section.
(d) Supervision of preparation of student reports and mark lists.
(e) Liaison with: Course Tutors
Other Section Leaders
College Agencies (Careers etc) and
External Organizations.
(f) Assistance with timetable.
(g) Responsibility for ordering material and equipment for courses.
(h) Keeping accounts of expenditure, if appropriate.
(i) Holding regular meetings of Section and reporting to Head of Department.
(j) Assistance in departmental duties as agreed with the Head of Department.

College B. SECTION LEADER

Is responsible to the Head or Deputy Head for a complete particular section of work and/or courses.

Will be specifically responsible in this area for general supervision of teaching staff covering the courses, advising on appointments and promotions, for non-teaching staff in laboratories/workshops/practical rooms in the section, for students within the courses of the section, for courses and classes, and for making out orders for apparatus, equipment and consumable materials for that section. He will advise the Head on all other matters relevant to the work of the section, namely, allocation of individual time-tables and duties of teaching staff, recommending appointment of part-time staff, time-tabling of classes, recommending capital items of equipment, putting forward financial estimates for the efficient operation of the section, maintaining contact with firms and other outside organizations connected with the work of the section and preparing that part of the prospectus relevant to the section, also leaflets and other publicity material for the section.

and when he was absent for one year from the college interviews were held in abeyance. It is important to note that in all three cases the colleges were small, having no more than 150 staff.

In all four colleges where heads of department conducted the interviews documents for use in the interview had been drawn up - in two cases by the staff development committee. The format of these varied, as did the topics to be covered (see Items 4.4 and 4.5). It should be noted that the second Item was under discussion at the time of our investigation. It is of interest, however, since it places strong emphasis on the teacher's own assessment of requirements and provides a slip for information on training opportunities. In all colleges the purpose of the interview was to discuss staff's needs for further training and/or experience rather than to review current performance. It was a feature of the approach taken that the onus was upon staff to identify their own needs; it was not seen as the interviewer's role to delineate these. The extent to which staff received guidance and help in making such assessments appeared to vary both between and within colleges.

Although in the seven colleges interviews were said to be 'informal', in all but two cases details of the interview are recorded and placed 'on file'. Where documents had been devised for use in the interview, a section (usually half a page) was included for the recording of points arising from the interview. Access to these records was limited to designated senior staff and the individual concerned. Upon the introduction of development interviews in one college, staff were granted the right to destroy their own records, should they so wish. The most important element of the record in all colleges was seen to be that part which described the course of action agreed upon in the discussion.

Where heads of department carried out the interviewing the major outcome of the interview was seen as being the drafting of a training programme. However, it was stressed that such plans had to be provisional and it was pointed out that lack of resources often prevented needs being met. For this reason some heads felt that interviews were dysfunctional because staff might have their expectations raised but not fulfilled. In particular it was felt that established members of staff who were 'not extreme cases' were most likely to find that a planned course of training could not be implemented. In the majority of instances it appeared that it was the responsibility of the individual concerned 'to follow up'

Item 4.4

STAFF DEVELOPMENT

Annual Notes on Staff Development for ....

Department ....

Head of Department and individual members of staff
should take the following points into account when holding discussions on staff development needs. These are
listed in no order of priority and need not be posed as
direct questions.

1. What training courses have been attended in the past
   five years?

2. What responsibilities had you in addition to your
   teaching commitment, its preparation and follow up,
   and how long do you spend each week on these additional responsibilities?

3. Is there any area where you feel more is asked of
   you than should be?

4. In what ways were your qualifications and abilities
   underused during the past year?

5. In what ways was the past year's development
   satisfactory and unsatisfactory?

6. Do you have effective professional advice from your
   senior colleagues to meet specific teaching needs?

7. Are you able to have regular contact with colleagues
   who take the same classes as you, in other subjects?

8. Have you any suggestions for improving the back-up
   services and teaching aids in your subject?

9. Are there any proposed courses that you know of,
   which you would like to attend next year?
   a) from the college internal list, for staff
      development.
   b) outside the college.

10. Are there any courses or activities you would like
    to attend if they were available?

11. What developments inside and outside the college are
    likely to affect the individual members of staff?

Brief notes (including agreed recommendations for Staff
Development for the year)

                    Signed: Lecturer................

Date ....
                    Head of Department................

Item 4.5

STAFF DEVELOPMENT FILE

Name_____ Dept_____

Grade_____ Date_____

The following checklist is intended to help you look at
the job you do in order to decide:

a) Parts of your job in which you feel competent.

b) Parts of your job where you would like to increase
   your knowledge/expertise.

c) Those parts of the job you would like to spend more
   time in doing.

It is not an exhaustive list, but it is a means of
starting to think about what you enjoy doing most, and
what you want from your work. Feel free to add to it
if you wish.

	I would like to know more about/become more experienced in	I would like to spend more time doing
Classroom teaching		
Practical Classes		
Writing Learning Objectives		
Curriculum Development		
Writing TEC/BEC units		
Use of A-V Aids		
Tutorial skills		
Selection/Testing of Students		
Teaching 'Low Level' Student		
First Aid Course		
Timetabling		
Ordering of equipment/materials		
Further Education Administration		
Estimates - Dept. preparation		
Control of equipment		
Supervision of Workshops, Labs.		
Writing Schemes of Assessment		
Planning Short Courses		
Preparation of New Courses		
Committee Membership		
Writing a Job application		
Interviewing techniques		
Other:		

Signed:_____   _____

      Member of Staff   Head of Department

Where the above includes some form of in-service training
requirement then the slip below should be forwarded to the
Chairman of the Staff Development and Research Committee.

Name_____ Department_____ Date_____

Please supply information/course details to the above on:

the decisions reached.

In all seven colleges performance assessment, as distinct from a discussion of training requirements, took place through informal methods as described earlier.

The majority of teachers within the seven colleges had accepted the introduction of staff development interviews and little opposition was voiced against them. Younger, more junior and more recently appointed teachers, however, tended to regard interviews more favourably than older, more senior and longer serving members of staff. On the whole the opportunity to discuss training possibilities and future career aspirations was welcomed. Additionally a widespread opinion was that regular discussions helped to promote better communication within the college. Nevertheless, in all colleges it was felt that some improvements needed to be made to the scheme as it was presently operating. Criticisms made by staff related to: the timing of the interview; the interviewer; and interview outcomes. In five colleges staff reported that their interviews were not always held within the specified time period. In colleges where the principal or vice-principal was involved in interviewing, younger and more junior staff tended to believe that discussion would be less inhibited if the head of department or section leader undertook this responsibility. It was typically argued that 'The present interviews are of value since they are private and the senior staff are friendly people, but response to one's professional superiors is always affected by their position as possible makers or breakers. A free interchange may not be easy'. Furthermore, teachers commonly stated that by virtue of the vice-principal's or principal's position in the hierarchy he could not be in possession of complete information (for instance, with regard to individual personality and domestic circumstances) to be able to perform the role effectively. The majority of staff in all colleges expressed some dissatisfaction that the interviews did not render more positive results: the interviews were 'a matter of going through the motions'. A common complaint was that although agreement had been reached on a course of action, in the event this had not materialized. This was reported by teachers who said that changes in timetables and responsibilities had been proposed as well as by those who intended to pursue further qualifications. A minority of teachers suggested that in the current economic climate, where there was a lack of finance for development, there was little point in holding interviews to discuss needs. The majority of teachers, however,

thought the system was worth retaining even if it failed
to help their own personal development as it offered the
opportunity for them to make known to management their
views and aspirations and enabled the head or principal/
vice-principal to get to know his or her staff better.

'Ideal' methods of assessment

The questionnaire distributed in the early stages of the
investigation asked staff to state the ideal method of
assessing teachers' needs. While 10 per cent of the
respondents saw no method as being ideal 75 per cent
supplied details of how this might be achieved (15 per
cent either did not know or supplied no information).
From the supplementary information which teachers provided it was evident that the majority clearly favoured the
employment of formal methods to assess requirements.
Both questionnaire and interview data showed that there
was little variation in the extent of support for formal
procedures between staff of different grades, although
on the whole it was the younger teachers in particular
who tended to favour such an approach. Differences were
exhibited, however, in the pattern of response found
between the colleges. In two, the majority of staff
opposed any formal method; the highest levels of support
being found in those colleges where interviews with
senior staff already occurred.

Of all the 'ideal' procedures suggested, 'discussions
with senior staff' received most widespread support
despite the difficulties involved. Although considerably
less popular, 'observation of teaching' was the second
most frequently mentioned method, while student assessment was the only other procedure proposed to any extent.
A small minority of teachers thought that the ideal
system should incorporate all three on the basis that a
variety of methods were required to investigate different
spheres of need. As one teacher commented: 'Interviews
with senior staff might help in those areas where I know
I am lacking; observation of my teaching would help where
I am not aware of any deficiencies - as would student
reaction'.

It was argued by those members of staff proposing the
observation method that, since the majority of teachers
in FE spend a major proportion of their time teaching,
staff development requirements would generally relate to
the classroom situation. Therefore the most appropriate
means of identifying needs was by evaluating 'on the job
performance'. As we doubted the extent to which observation would be generally acceptable to FE staff, we

explored the question further in interviews and sought
teachers reactions to this method. Contrary to our expectations, slightly over half said that they would not
object to classroom observation. It was evident that a
number of teachers were prepared to accept this because
they had previously been observed while undertaking a
course of initial teacher training. Craft teachers in
particular pointed out that they had little anxiety regarding observation *per se* as currently colleagues and
technicians might in any case be present when classes
were conducted. A similar point was made by teachers of
other subjects who engaged in team teaching. A major
factor, however, which emerged regarding the acceptability of formal observation was teachers' belief that this
already occurred but took place covertly. It was widely
reported that senior staff 'looked through windows' and
'dropped into classes'. It was seen as desirable to
bring this activity 'into the open' and to so structure
it that it could be beneficial to the teachers themselves,
enabling them to receive some feedback on their teaching.
It was considered that present methods were unreliable
and might be unjust in that they provided little opportunity for the teacher to explain and justify his or her
approach.

Nevertheless it was acknowledged that implementing a
formal system of observation would require solutions to
be found to three fundamental questions.

What form should observation take? Many teachers doubted
that it was in fact possible to avoid artificial situations being created. Although the majority believed that
they should be forewarned of visits, it was anticipated
that lessons might be 'specially prepared' and classes
'set up with students'. Often teachers recounted their
own experiences of this on teaching practice. It was
seen as imperative that observation take place regularly
and assessment not be made on the basis of a limited
number of visits of short duration. Where a range of
classes was taught it was considered essential that the
teacher be viewed in a number of different classroom
situations.

What should be assessed? Few teachers made specific
recommendations regarding the criteria to be employed in
monitoring classroom performance. Those staff who did
offer suggestions often referred to the fact that criteria
were already in existence, since schemes had been drawn
up to evaluate trainee and probationary teachers. These
in the main were considered to be adequate. Aspects of
classroom teaching which it was proposed should be

assessed included: lesson preparation, classroom management, teaching method, use of audio-visual aids and handouts, and rapport with students. There was, however, a widespread view that although observers would be expected to agree upon excellent and very poor teaching, there might be considerable disparities in the evaluation of performances lying between these two extremes. Hence, the staff development requirements so identified could differ significantly. Teachers raising this issue tended to regard the standardization of evaluations as an insoluble problem.

Who should observe teaching? If heads of department were to undertake this task, it was felt essential for them to possess professional teaching qualifications. A number of teachers were adamant that they would not be prepared to accept assessments made by a head without a teaching certificate. In this context it is of interest to note that one principal commented at interview that, as he himself was untrained, he saw this as potentially acting against any judgement on teaching skills that he might make. It was also stated that even where heads were teacher-trained, they should be required to undergo some further training in 'identifying teaching skills' and in counselling techniques. There was some feeling that it would be best for observation to be carried out solely by a professional tutor or a lecturer in education. A few teachers, however, doubted that any 'ideal' observer could be found.

Teachers who proposed assessment by students often stated that they thought heads of department did take student opinion into account when evaluating a member of staff, even if this was not done on a formal basis. Our own findings indicate that this is indeed the case. In a number of departments attempts had been made by the head to obtain direct feedback from students. In one, GCE 'O' and 'A' level students are asked to complete a questionnaire relating to their course at the end of the first term. In another, a new head had instituted a system whereby all full-time students meet in groups of five with the head of department or his deputy to discuss their work. Samples of their class and homework and of handouts provided by their teachers are also brought to this meeting.

Teachers favouring this method of assessment frequently mentioned that they themselves already elicited student opinion, and in a number of cases questionnaires had been designed for this purpose. The results were generally considered to be helpful, particularly in avoiding similar 'pitfalls' the following year. As one teacher observed 'students are far more perceptive and realistic than we give them credit for'. It was argued that even where teachers did not systematically obtain assessment by students, they would tend to be aware of students' evaluations. For instance, it was commonly mentioned that 'students vote with their feet' and that no teacher could be 'totally ignorant of student reaction and response' to their classes. The latter point is graphically illustrated in the following comment made by one teacher: 'I know my presentation is monotonous because my students have told me so, and in any case I can see when their eyes start to close. I am consciously trying to do something about this'.

Student assessment tended to be proposed as the 'ideal' method by younger and more junior staff. Their main argument was that students are in the best position to judge a teacher, as they see him or her on a daily basis. It was pointed out that this may be a more realistic impression than that gained from an occasional visit by an observer, and that in any case 'students are consumers and have the right to make their views known'. It was thought that because of the problems involved and the anticipated resistance to it by some staff, FE managers had neglected to make use of a valuable means by which the quality of teaching could be improved. In the words of one teacher: 'Assessment by students is long overdue but everyone avoids this issue'. Staff who rejected this approach tended to be quite vehement in their opposition arguing variously that: students do not have the experience to comment; they could not be objective and would be swayed by lecturer attitudes to punctuality and standards of marking; they would not be able to judge 'the content' of lectures; their evaluations would be affected by the personality and popularity of the lecturer. Such teachers were, moreover, likely to point to the difficulty of using student assessment without breaching professional ethics. Some staff, while questioning whether 16-19 year-old students were sufficiently mature, thought that older students' views might be helpful. In a similar vein, whereas evaluation by non-advanced students was often opposed, assessment by students taking advanced courses was more acceptable.

Perhaps surprisingly, few other methods of assessing staffdevelopment needs were proposed. Only three - peer assessment, team teaching and self assessment - appeared to have any measure of support. Team teaching, it was thought, could help to create a supportive climate so that evaluations could be expressed which were not

threatening to the teacher. It was also thought that
teachers' own awareness of their strengths and weaknesses
was likely to be increased, as they could compare their
performance with that of others. Another perceived
advantage was that assessments would be made by colleagues
who were aware of the problems and difficulties of teaching particular groups of students. Thus their observations were likely to be 'more realistic' than those made
by a head of department or another observer. Essentially,
teachers who favoured this method saw it as providing
the opportunity for 'constructive criticism' - something
which was regarded as generally absent from staff development interviews.

Career Counselling

There was widespread feeling in all but one of the
colleges that existing provision for career counselling
was inadequate. Even where staff development interviews
took place staff did not perceive them as counselling
sessions. Where professional tutors had been appointed,
staff tended to feel that it was more appropriate to
approach them on training matters than on questions relating specifically to their career. Teachers who expressed the desire for career counselling were usually
in early and mid-career; some of them now questioned
whether they had made the 'right' choice of occupation,
but did not feel that they could voice such doubts in
interviews with either heads of department or vice-
principals/principals without jeopardising their position
within the college. Significantly, in the one college
where the majority of staff were satisfied with existing
counselling provision, interviews were held by the
principal who specifically described them as providing
him with the chance to offer career counselling.

With the creation of professional tutor posts it would
appear that many FE colleges would now be in a good
position, if they so wished, to introduce a formal system
of career counselling. Certainly our study indicates
that a demand exists for such a service, and professional
tutors themselves would favour such a development. Several
teachers, in fact, suggested that they would like to see
interviews regularly scheduled between the tutor and staff
members, considering that this would be preferable to the
present arrangement in which the individual initiates the
contact.

A scheme being piloted in an LEA in which one of the study
colleges is located would seem worthy of consideration on
a wider scale. The Authority (which employs well over
2,000 full-time FE teachers, many of whom have long

periods of service) introduced a Staff Advisory/Counsell-
ing service in 1979. It was envisaged that this service
would: strengthen the links betwen the various educational institutions and the wider working community, as
some of the counsellors were to be drawn from industry
and commerce; add a new supportive and complementary
dimension to current individual college provision; and
provide a means for harmonizing personal staff aspirations with individual college strategy and LEA policy.
The scheme, which operates on a voluntary basis, provides
staff development advice, activity and information. While
the scheme is co-ordinated from County Hall, it operates
under the general control of a Steering Committee com-
prising representatives of the local university and
polytechnic, the colleges, industry and other interested
groups. Each adviser/counsellor is allotted a number of
clients who, on a self-referral basis, are offered
consultative facilities for such periods of time as the
clients themselves may consider necessary.

Overview

Altnough in twelve of the nineteen colleges, no systematic procedures existed to assess staff development
needs, it was commonly believed by teachers in these
institutions that their work was nevertheless being
evaluated. This was seen to be taking place on an *ad
hoc* and informal basis, providing little, if any, opportunity for feedback related to staff development. Where
formal schemes *had* been instituted it was not widely
believed by teachers that these were effective in evaluating their requirements. Of particular significance
here is the fact that, although staff development interviews were usually held, job descriptions were not
routinely discussed (or amended) nor were teachers'
strengths and weaknesses necessarily reviewed. While
interviews were seldom regarded by staff as having tang-
ible outcomes, the majority of teachers still wanted the
system to be retained and even called for interviews to
be neld more frequently. This would suggest that tne
interviews perform other functions: they offer the
opportunity for two-way communcation and may serve to
reassure staff that they nave not been overlooked within
the organization.

Given that in all nineteen colleges heavy emphasis was
placed on lecturers' identifying tneir own needs, it is
hardly surprising that existing schemes were often regarded as failing to involve some of those who might
receive particular benefit from staff development activities. It would seem that staff may well need help in

determining their own requirements, since not everyone can analyse his or her own performance objectively.

Moreover, self-assessment may be especially unreliable, when, as was frequently reported, staff feel that their promotion prospects may be reduced if they draw management's attention to perceived weaknesses. It would thus seem that total reliance should not be placed on teachers' self-identification of requirements and that other methods of assessing need are called for.

It staff development activities are to relate closely to individual need, performance will have to be assessed. Senior staff will therefore need to pay attention to how, and by whom, performance is to be evaluated – difficult though this may be. The opinions of staff will have to be sought, since schemes are only viable to the extent that teachers are prepared to take part in them. Our findings suggest that it would be wrong to assume that staff will inevitably be antagonistic to formal assessment. Nevertheless, it should be noted that although more than half of those interviewed said they would not object to classroom observation, it was evident that many considered it unacceptable for this to be undertaken by heads of department, especially if they were not teacher trained. In any event it would seem undesirable for assessments to be based solely on evaluations formulated by one person alone, and there would appear to be much to recommend assessments which take into account the views of other colleagues and students. Whatever type of scheme is introduced, it is essential that it be accompanied by provision for counselling in general, and career counselling in particular.

CHAPTER 5

Professional tutors

Background

In Britain the idea of a school-based professional tutor
came to national prominence after the publication of the
James Report (1972). The concept may, however, be
traced back to American experiments in the late 1960s,
which demonstrated the efficacy of delegating to a
practising teacher the task of introducing and sustain-
ing colleagues' support for innovatory school practices
(Watkins, 1978). Reflecting the developments which had
taken place in the school sector, the ACSTT Report (1975)
recommended that there should be at least one professional tutor in every FE college on either a full- or
part-time basis, who would normally be a member of the
full-time staff of the college. Such personnel, it was
anticipated, would form a key element in the implementation of the proposed arrangements for in-service
training. In broad terms the ACSTT Subcommittee considered that 'a professional tutor should be a counsellor
of teachers, maintain liaison with training centres and
others involved in the training process, and assist in
the induction of new teachers and the further training
of the staff as a whole' (Ibid, p16).

At national, regional and local levels reactions to the
ACSTT proposal have varied considerably. In their responses to DES Circular 11/77 several RACs remained unconvinced of the need for such an appointment, while
others, although supporting the recommendation in principle, questioned whether it would be possible to fund
such posts. Five of the RACs nevertheless expressed a
high level of commitment to the concept and in at least
one region the target of one professional tutor in
every college had almost been reached. In those Councils
who submitted regional schemes incorporating professional
tutors the responsibilities of such staff were seen to

vary widely in scope; from an involvement in 'the over-
lapping areas of personnel management, staff development,
teaching effectiveness and curriculum development' to a
more restricted role confined to supporting new teachers.

The ACFHE/APTI Report (1973) stated that one of the essential requirements of a staff development policy was
that a member of staff should be made responsible for
staff development and be designated the Staff Development Officer. It was advocated that in large colleges
(with approximately 250 staff) there should be a SDO
appointed at the principal lecturer or senior lecturer
level, but that in smaller colleges the vice-principal
might well function in this capacity, though it was considered preferable that a separate position be created.
In the event many colleges, regardless of size, adopted
the expedient of designating the (or a) vice-principal
as SDO. This is hardly surprising since traditionally
the VP has been expected to take overall charge of work
related to staff training. It is, however, questionable whether this was a wise choice. By virtue of his
administrative commitments alone, it would seem unlikely
that the vice-principal can perform all of the functions
envisaged for a professional tutor. As the ACFHE/APTI
Working Party pointed out, this work 'can often be, and
usually is, a time-consuming business' (Ibid, p16).
Additionally, his status in the hierarchy could (as was
seen in Chapter 4) render him unacceptable to staff as a
career counsellor.

Since neither the ACSTT nor the ACFHE/APTI Reports
offered detailed descriptions of the duties to be performed, it was evident that there would be much scope
for individual interpretation of the professional tutor
role. Thus it might be anticipated that in practice considerable diversity would be found in the manner in which
roles were negotiated and operationalised. This indeed
proved to be the case in our study.

Appointments in the 19 colleges

In the initial stages of this investigation information
was sought from all principals regarding the members of
staff in their colleges who had responsibilities in the
staff development area. This section briefly outlines
their responses.

Twelve of the nineteen principals indicated that their
colleges had professional tutors, while in the remaining
seven no individual was seen as acting in this capacity.
Only in six colleges was it indicated that the tutors

had a wide range of staff development commitments of the
kind illustrated in the two job descriptions presented
as Items 5.1 and 5.2. In the other six cases duties were
narrowly defined.

In three of the six colleges where professional tutors
had an extended role overall responsibility for staff
development rested with the vice-principal, although in
only one case was he given the title SDO. In this instance the professional tutor is 'concerned with the
professional needs of the teaching staff in the context
of the aims of staff development' and 'acts as an academic
counsellor to individual members of the teaching staff on
matters which may affect the quality of their teaching',
while the SDO 'advises on the resource implications of
policy, sanctions absence and financial support for
courses and acts as the chairman of the staff development committee'. In a further two colleges there were
staff known as SDOs, but their status and duties differed
significantly from that described above. They were
members of the teaching staff who were expected to provide a link between the professional tutor and the
departments and, in particular, to keep their colleagues
informed of the staff development opportunities open to
them. The SDO job description used in one of these
colleges is reproduced below as Item 5.3.

Item 5.1

The Professional Tutor is concerned with two broad areas
of activity:-
A Staff Development Function:

To advise on the various means of developing the teaching
skills and professional knowledge of individual members
of staff in relation to departmental objectives and staffing arrangements and also in respect of the needs of the
individual member of staff as identified within the
College programme for Staff Development.

a) In relation to full-time and part-time members of staff,
   to advise on the facilities available for, or necessary
   to, the improvement of professional expertise and
   teaching skills, with particular emphasis on the needs
   of the College staff.

b) To advise and assist the Principal and Heads of Departments to develop the potential of individual members
   of staff in relation to (a) above.

c) To advise the College administration on areas of staff
   development which might usefully be offered on the
   campus in support of the College Staff Development

Programme.

d) To assist with the implementation of staff development arrangements and, in particular, with regard
to new members of staff, to assist with induction
arrangements and monitoring of classroom performance
and the use of audio-visual and other sorts of
teaching aid.

e) To liaise with the various College interests (other
individuals or groups having a Staff Development
Function). The Tutor will be an ex-officio member of
the Staff Development Committee with responsibility
for monitoring the implementation of that Committees
recommendations.

f) To liaise with the College Librarian in the task of
maintaining an up-to-date record of outside courses
relating to Staff Development and to advise Heads of
Departments of any new provision which could be
relevant to their subject responsibilities.

A Teaching Function:

The Tutor will participate in teaching in those areas in
which she has special qualifications and experience.

Location:

The Professional Tutor's Office is in the main Administration Building on the first floor (staircase next to
Library Building). The Tutor will normally be available
except for regular teaching and other commitments;
(these times are posted outside the office). Contact
may be made independently or through the Heads of Department or the Departmental Staff Development representative.

Programme:

From time to time the tutor will organise seminars and
short courses for teachers and these will be in conjunction with the Staff Development Committee's arrangements
for internal courses.

Item 5.2

The Professional Tutor will be directly responsible to
the Principal and will have no departmental administrative
duties. He will attend the Academic Board by invitation
and be a member of the Staff Development Committee under
the chairmanship of the Vice Principal. When matters
relating to staff training are on the Agenda he will also
attend the Heads of Departments' Meetings by invitation.

The Professional Tutor will be directly responsible to the Principal for:

1) The planning and implementation of a programme of lecture seminars or tutorials for the effective induction of newly appointed academic staff.

2) The personal oversight of newly appointed academic staff during their first year of appointment.

3) The occasional support and assistance of the established academic staff in the teaching situation.

4) The planning, implementation and/or co-ordination of a programme of lectures, seminars, tutorials and group discussions to serve the development needs of the existing academic staff at all levels.

5) The oversight of academic staff members on secondment to extended courses away from the college.

6) To supervise the operation of a central resource workshop for the use of all academic staff.

Job Objectives

1) To aid newly appointed academic staff to settle into the college working environment and contribute effectively to the teaching programmes and the cultural life of the college.

2) To encourage the development of more effective learning situations by means of:
   a) Inter-staff discussion and exchange of ideas
   b) encouraging and assisting self appraisal of teaching effectiveness
   c) providing opportunity for the up-dating of personal subject knowledge
   d) planned, co-ordinated and assessed experimental teaching programmes
   e) encouraging and developing the effective use of resources

3) To promote and co-ordinate continuing academic staff development in the form of:
   a) inter-staff discussion and exchange of ideas
   b) a programme of visiting lecturers
   c) attendance at conferences etc and publication of reports resulting from attendance
   d) attendance at external courses
   e) circulation of selected published data
   f) effective usage of library and other existing resources
   g) development of new resources

Man Profile

To be effective as staff tutor the person appointed to the post of Professional Tutor should have, in some measure, many or all of the following personal qualifications or attributes:

1) Extensive teaching experience with various age levels of student including, particularly, mature adults

2) Good organizational ability and organizational experience at a senior responsible level in the further education sector

3) The ability to develop good personal relationships with staff colleagues. In particular to engender trust and foster understanding of the tutor's role

4) A sound knowledge of production methods and the application of aids in the learning situation

5) An understanding of educational principles and method, both general and special

6) A knowledge of the structuring and administration of the further/higher education service

7) Sympathy for the educational needs of students

8) Understanding of the problems facing teachers in the classroom situation. A sympathetic approach to the solution of these problems

9) Awareness for the need for curriculum review and development

Salary: Principal Lecturer Grade

Item 5.3

Departmental Staff Development Officer

1. To hold regular counselling sessions with new staff.

2. To visit new staff in class on a regular basis.

3. To keep a list of visits and counselling sessions for (1) and (2).

4. To keep Head of Department informed of Staff Development activities in the College and Department.

5. To publicise Education and Staff Development work in the Department.

6. To actively promote staff development courses etc.

7. To advise and help all staff in the department.

8. To identify common teaching problems so that resources can be brought to bear on them.

9. Attend regular meetings of Staff Development Officers.

10. Record all Staff Development activities on Department.

11. To obtain feedback on the effectiveness of Staff Development courses and other activities so that these courses can be improved.

12. To monitor progress of staff on external courses, with particular reference to the value of the course and its contribution to the work of the College.

13. To keep up to date lists of all people engaged in work connected with staff development in th e College - on internal courses, external courses, short courses.

In the six colleges where the professional tutor role was more restricted in scope, the tutors' main responsibilities related to induction and initial teacher training, although in some cases additional responsibilities were specified. In one college, for example, the tutor was present at the staff development interviews held with the vice-principal. It was quite common to find that the 'restricted' professional tutor role was being performed by lecturers in education (often two or three in each college) who were granted an average of two hours per week class contact remission for their staff development work. In one such case the principal noted that 'the teacher responsible for teacher training courses effectively performs the role of a professional tutor' but that 'her position has not been formalized as such because of the reluctance on the part of several heads of department to accept the interference with their own function which they saw as implied by such an appointment'.

None of the remaining seven colleges had professional tutors, but in three of them the principals were of the opinion that such an appointment ought to be made. They were hoping for a change in local authority policy which would enable them to carry through their plans in this area. Despite this, all seven colleges had staff with specific responsibilities for the development of their colleagues.

In one college members of the staff development committee were regarded as 'carrying out much of the work of a professional tutor'. In another, responsibility was vested in a principal lecturer who was responsible directly to the principal 'for all personnel matters'. Additionally, two of the college's senior lecturers assist with a County In-Service Cert.Ed. scheme operate CGLI courses and 'help and advise new teaching staff'.

Of particular interest in this context is a college where the principal himself is actively involved in staff development and is, moreover, of the opinion that this duty should not be delegated. He argued against the need to appoint a professional tutor on the grounds that this work enables him to come into contact with as many of his staff as possible; that staff development is far too important to be left to a middle or junior member of staff; that the leadership of any unit implies an involvement with the development of its members; that the job is already being carried out efficiently by a support services unit, which assists him with back-up information on staff development policy and practice.

Tutors with an extended role

The James Report (1972) recommended that in large schools 'he (the tutor) should be recognised and paid as a major head of department' (p37). In line with this recommendation three of the tutors performing an extended role had been appointed as principal lecturers. The other three were senior lecturers, and such a level of appointment was seen by them as appropriate. Although two tutors were the leaders of small education divisions, none were members of a department. Rather, they were all directly responsible either to the principal or vice-principal. All felt that this was the most satisfactory arrangement, their collective response being summed up by one tutor who said 'the professional tutor is a college man; definitely non-departmental'. Where, then, did the tutors' allegiance lie, given that they had unique status within the college? While four maintained that they attempted to adopt a 'neutral stance' (avoiding being identified either with management or the rank and file) two felt strongly that their first loyalty was to the teaching staff – in the words of one tutor, he was 'the prisoners' friend'. Emphasizing that his intention was not to be seen as part of management, this tutor reported that he avoided being involved or associated with any activities which might prejudice his contact and personal relationships with teaching staff.

Two tutors reported that they had had to overcome some initial hostility from staff. In one college the professional tutor, on taking up the post, was met with a NATFHE branch memorandum to members which advised: 'Please collect all up-to-date information re the work and activity of Mr ... insofar as he may have contacted your department. There is evidence of an unhealthy situation developing. Please alert all lecturers to the fact that they need not admit anyone to have a look at

their teaching save their head of department, and further
advise colleagues not to commit themselves to co-operate
with Mr ... until we know the results of a request I have
put to the principal for an urgent interview on this
matter'. After discussions referred to in the memorandum,
the tutor's role and responsibilities were clarified.
From this experience the individual concerned concluded:
'Staff must be well informed before the post is made and
as it devolves in order to avoid anxieties on the part
of the teaching staff... I don't look over my shoulder
so much nowadays'. This tutor was new to the college,
which may in part explain why staff had such fears.
Only one other of the tutors was an external appointment
the remaining four having been members of the college
staff before taking up their present position.

The professional tutors also thought it vital that issues
relating to their own functions vis-a-vis the heads of
department were resolved before they took up office: 'A
professional tutor should not be foisted on a college.
The way should be paved so that he's not considered as a
threat to the traditional voice of a VP/HOD but complementary and above all a help to staff'; 'Before anyone
is introduced to a college (as PT) there must be a preparatory exercise involving discussions, particularly
with HODs, on whose territory you might be encroaching
and whose role might seem to be vulnerable'.

It was stressed that their job could only be done with
the support of the heads of department: 'If the professional tutor is going to enjoy the confidence of the
heads - and he must - then he has to be a tool that they
can use. If he (HOD) hears that any teacher is having
some kind of problem, he must go to that teacher and tell
them about the professional tutor who can offer advice
and help'. One tutor, however, estimated that it may
take up to five years to be accepted by the heads.

All professional tutors were responsible for their
college's induction programme and had teaching commitments
on it. It was agreed that one of their primary functions
was to provide support for new members of staff. Their
involvement with induction was seen by them to be
beneficial in establishing contact with new teachers and
affording an early opportunity to draw their attention to
provisions made within the college for staff development.
Four of the tutors also had responsibility for organizing
and teaching on the CGLI 730 course offered by their
college (in the remaining two cases this was not run at
the college). Three had, in addition, been involved in
establishing a CNAA Cert.Ed. course and reported that

they had participated in the planning and writing of the submission prior to lecturing on the course. All tutors stated that they were expected to organize in-house short courses. While in three cases it was the staff development committee which suggested the subjects to be included in short course programmes, in the other colleges this was the responsibility of the tutor. Only two tutors had any additional teaching commitments within their own subject areas (in one case, English and Social Science and in the other Health Education). One, in particular, varied his commitments from year to year to enable him to come into contact with staff in as many departments as possible.

All tutors with an extended role saw it as an important part of their job to make sure that information on courses, conferences and activities were circulated. As one remarked: 'The dissemination of information is at the root of the whole enterprise... It is often received far too late... The fact that somebody is there collecting all this information every morning and directing it where it really belongs and where people can make use of it is absolutely vital'. It was common for tutors to maintain an up-to-date directory of courses available and to keep staff development records which enabled them to identify the special interests of individual lecturers. All tutors stated that they were available to advise teachers on applications for conferences, courses and secondment. Only two were directly involved in the processing of staff applications for financial support, remission and secondment.

Tutors were, however, divided regarding whether or not it was appropriate for them to adopt an overt approach to staff and recommend that they 'should develop'. Moreover, tutors found it difficult to generalize on this issue, since much was seen to depend on individual circumstances. Even those tutors who espoused a non-directive approach thought that there might be occasions, for example when a teacher was experiencing difficulties, when the tutor should approach the lecturer concerned and initiate a discussion of his or her problems. In this situation it was felt that it might be necessary to recommend a particular course of action; in general it was considered preferable for teachers themselves to be responsible for evaluating their own needs and deciding upon the most appropriate strategy for meeting them. One tutor put his own view as follows: 'You can only go so far. After that you work within the college infrastructure and make it known to every member of staff that they must also have an obligation to develop themselves. I throw the

onus as much as I possibly can back to staff; I let them
see that they can't just sit back and wait for somebody
to develop them'. In another tutor's opinion 'One volunteer is worth 12 pressed men'.

Indeed it was believed that an interventionist approach
could be counterproductive. In the long run it was considered that more might be achieved by creating a climate
within the college which increases teachers' conscious-
ness of their own needs. One way in which this might be
achieved is for the tutor to ensure that he or she is in
regular contact with the college staff. Informal meetings with teachers were therefore regarded as being invaluable for the opportunities they created of increasing awareness of staff development in general and
providing the chance for teachers to raise issues worrying
them.

In addition it was seen as important that the tutor should
sit on a variety of college committees. Such involvement
would not only increase the tutor's own understanding of
the dynamics of the college but would also help ensure
that the training implications of any matters discussed
were considered. In particular, it was thought desirable
that the tutor should be on the Academic Board, and five
of the six tutors were, in fact, members. In one case,
a college working party set up prior to the tutor's
appointment argued thus in favour of his inclusion:
'curriculum development and staff development could not
be divorced and since one of the prime functions of the
Academic Board was curriculum development it was important that the Professional Tutor was a member of the Board'.

Staff counselling was regarded by the tutors as potentially one of the most vital aspects of their role. Five of
the six reported that they had major commitments in this
area and emphasized that it was important that teachers
should feel able to discuss any matter in the knowledge
that confidentiality would be assured. However, one of
these tutors pointed out that she tended to be largely
involved with counselling part-time staff since few full-
time staff contacted her in this context.

There was general agreement that it was not possible to
concentrate solely on 'training matters' since these are
frequently inextricably linked to a teacher's personal
circumstances. Not only did tutors report that staff consulted them on personal matters, such as marital problems,
but that they might also be involved by virtue of a
referral from a senior member of staff. It was pointed
out that even where teachers had consulted the tutor with

regard to an application for a course, this exchange
could lead to the introduction and discussion of personal
worries and anxieties. None of the tutors stated that
they based their approach on a particular model of counselling; rather they described their role in terms of
'lending an ear' or 'being willing to listen'.

With one exception, the tutors considered that it was not
possible to maintain a counselling role together with any
involvement in an appraisal scheme. None of the colleges
in which the tutors worked had, in fact, introduced a
formal appraisal system, but in one case such a scheme is
under discussion and the tutor anticipates that, if this
is implemented he will be required to take on some work
in this area. All, nevertheless, recognised the dangers
of participation and all but one also voiced strong opposition to the idea that the tutor should contribute in
any way to the discussion of staff promotions. All the
tutors reported observing classroom teaching, though in
some cases this was restricted to inductees and to
teachers taking the CGLI 730 and CNAA Cert.Ed. courses;
not all made their evaluations of such teachers known to
heads of department. Two of the tutors stated that they
would observe established members of staff, if requested
by their heads of department to do so, and would in such
circumstances report back their assessments. Instances
of this occurring were however cited as being 'few and
far between'. One of these tutors stressed that he had
decided to do so because at his college heads do sit in
on the classes of teachers experiencing difficulties.
He felt therefore that his presence provides the opportunity for another viewpoint to be forwarded - in his
words 'at least the HOD may have his own impression
verified or challenged'. Those tutors who were not prepared to undertake such activities felt strongly that
this was not their brief.

Three of the tutors had supervisory responsibilities for
the college's audio-visual aids. All tutors also undertook some further duties which related specifically to
their own college context.

Tutors with a restricted role

In the three colleges where the title 'professional
tutor' was not officially applied, tutors pointed to the
difficulty of attempting to perform their role. It was
considered that if colleges were to conform to the 'spirit'
of the ACSTT Report (1975) then tutors must be designated
officially and their functions clarified. In addition it
was argued that if tutors' responsibilities were not to

be restricted to induction and teacher training then remission from classroom teaching 'needed to be realistic' to enable such work to be undertaken. In the other three colleges, where the title of professional tutor was officially employed, tutors queried whether they were, in fact, professional tutors since they were only in part fulfilling the role as envisaged in the ACSTT Report. Crucially, these staff in all six colleges saw themselves less as professional tutors than as 'teacher trainers'.

Without exception, staff referred to as professional tutors had duties related to induction and teacher training programmes. In the main such staff had responsibities for, and taught on, the CGLI 730 and, where these were offered, CGLI 731 and 732 courses. All participated in the running of in-service, in-house courses although these tended to be of only two or three days duration. Exceptionally, one tutor had organized a programme (one afternoon session a week for six weeks) for heads of department. This had been arranged in response to the ACSTT (1978) discussion paper on education management and has been provided in conjunction with the local college of education (technical). As has been previously noted one tutor attended staff development interviews held by the vice-principal. Though four of these tutors sat on their college's Academic Board, their membership resulted from their status as a teacher representative rather than from their training role within the college. Although none of these staff members circulated information on courses and conferences to teachers directly, it was stated in five colleges that there was an education division which held such information available for staff consultation. No further commitments in the area of staff development were mentioned. In general it was asserted that heavy teaching timetables inhibited a wider training involvement.

Views of other staff members

In four of the six colleges where there were professional tutors who performed an extended role the vast majority of staff supported their tutor's appointment. He was seen as making a significant contribution to staff development in the college and heads of department in particular saw the incumbent as acting as a catalyst in this respect. Overall, there was little doubt in the minds of staff that there was a need for someone to act in this capacity: 'A lecturer working flat out on course work and administration seldom has the chance to consider how he or she might develop'; 'Staff development is now a very complicated field and experienced guidance is essential'.

The main functions of the tutors were seen by staff as:
conducting induction programmes, acting as adviser to
heads of department and teachers on new techniques and
aids, providing literature and information on courses,
and running in-service in-house courses. There was a
widespread feeling among staff that their tutor was
'approachable'. The majority of teachers who had consulted the tutor reported doing so to obtain information
on courses, conferences and application procedures. Few
teachers, however, indicated that they had sought counselling for teaching, vocational or personal problems.
Although heads of department said that they would refer
staff to the professional tutor, in no instance did they
state that they would consider approaching him regarding
their own development.

Little dissatisfaction was expressed by staff regarding
the professional tutors and indeed no major criticism
was made which applied to all four tutors. In two colleges, where the appointment of the tutors was more recent
some teachers did express resentment at the level of the
appointment. Often such teachers drew attention to the
fact that, as a consequence, 'there was one less senior
post'. Some new teachers were critical of the tutors'
approach to induction. A minority expressed the opinion
that the tutor should play a more active role in encouraging staff to refresh their teaching techniques and update their subject knowledge. It was felt that if
development was left up to the individual then there
would always be some teachers who would remain 'stuck in
their ruts'.

In the other two colleges, however, general criticism was
expressed of the tutors. In one, where the tutor and
vice-principal reported that the appointment arose from
an internal departmental reorganization, several members
of staff made reference to the manner in which the tutor
was appointed. As one head of department said 'the P/T
was not appointed altogether for the right reasons'.
This was seen as affecting attitudes to staff development. One teacher summed up the situation thus: 'We
have a full-time PT who works hard at it. But this
person was given the job as a 'kick sideways' after con-
spicuously failing in important work elsewhere. Hence
staff development cannot be taken seriously by those who
see it as something to employ this person's time and
energy... imagine the effects on the image of staff
development'. In the second college, a common complaint
was that the tutor was too passive in his approach to

staff development. Some teachers at interview even expressed surprise that he was, in fact, the college's
professional tutor, as they regarded him solely as a
lecturer in education. At interview our suggestion that
he might be approached regarding teaching or career
matters was frequently responded to with wry amusement.

In those colleges where professional tutors performed a
'restricted role' staff drew attention to the perceived
inadequacies of the present situation. Many did not feel
that they could turn either to a lecturer in education
or to their head of department for advice regarding their
teaching or career development. Given below are a selection of teachers' comments, representative of the arguments put forward in favour of a professional tutor being
appointed:

'For the past two years I have had great difficulty finding out what courses are offered, locally and nationally
and even within the local authority. We are forced to
rely on the department passing on to us such sources as
notifications, relevant journals, LEA newsletters etc,
and generally speaking this has simply not been done.'

'Any professional needs to keep in touch with current
developments in his field. A full-time staff development adviser could be a key element in this since
teachers do not have the time, energy or money to
successfully maintain their development on an individual
basis.'

'Many staff have problems of control or course development and work preparation. These could be dealt with on
a confidential basis without involving senior staff.'

'I feel it is essential to have someone outside the
department who can give considered, unbiased advice and
who is able to meet authority on an equal footing.'

Significantly, teachers who opposed such an appointment
seldom argued that the college already discharged its
responsibilities for staff development adequately. Instead the two major reasons provided against having a
professional tutor were that it was the responsibility
of the individual to develop himself and that the college
already had too many non-teaching posts.

In only one of the colleges with no professional tutor
did the majority of staff respond favourably to existing
personnel arrangements. Here the principal was actively
involved in and strongly committed to staff development
work. In this case only a small number of staff would
welcome the appointment of a professional tutor and these

tended to be younger, newly appointed teachers, who despite the principal's 'open door' policy did not feel, by virtue of his status, that they could consult him. Some teachers, however, asserted that they had difficulties in obtaining specific information on courses and conferences from the support services unit.

In all the remaining colleges without a professional tutor there was widespread support for the proposal that a professional tutor should be appointed, even where the vice-principal had been designated as the staff development officer. In general, staff within these colleges did not consider that heads of department were already fulfilling the functions advocated for a professional tutor - a point of view supported by some of the heads who favoured a tutor being appointed: 'There is never enough time to do enough. A busy HOD tends to be forced to regard staff development as assisting in the solution of urgent problems - and rarely has time to identify staff problems as preventing problems'; 'there are limits to how much you can load a HOD'; 'A professional tutor might do a better job than HODs since staff development would be his sole job'. Yet the strongest reaction against professional tutors was expressed by other heads of department in these colleges who maintained that it was the job of a head to be responsible for the professional development of his or her staff.

Professional tutor training

Reflecting the three-cycle approach of the James Committee, the ACSTT Report (1975, p16) recommended a three-stage training process for professional tutors:

Stage   I: Introductory (one-term or equivalent) task-centred courses

Stage II: Course of advanced study in education, eg Diploma in Advanced Study in Further Education with appropriate options, or Course of Advanced Study designed entirely to meet the specific needs of professional tutors, or M.Ed. with appropriate options

Stage III: Regular in-service training

Local authorities were urged to award high priority to Stage I and it was deemed desirable that Stage II should follow within three years of appointment. Yet, to date, very limited provision has been made. Only one of the tutors in this study had received any specific preparation for the role and the group as a whole were somewhat dismissive of the need for formal courses. Rather, they defined their needs as: 'requiring an opportunity for an interchange of views, experiences and methods with colleagues'; 'an opportunity for reflection out of the college environment'. It is not to be denied that discussions and seminars are of value. If however they are to be regarded as the sole vehicle for training, professional tutors may find that their own credibility as trainers and proponents of training is called into question by their clients.

The small number of professional tutor appointments made in recent years has militated against the introduction of any systematic training arrangement, but as more tutors are employed in FE, the demand for training schemes is likely to increase and courses may become a more viable proposition than they have been in the past: Garnett College reported that the part-time Diploma for Professional Tutors in Further Education was withdrawn in 1976 as a consequence of the low number of registrations for the course. Both tutors and those aspiring to such positions may need to be convinced of the desirability of formal training - and this will not be achieved if current or past courses are not perceived as sufficiently relevant to the tutors' situation. The Garnett course, for example, was thought by some tutors to have failed to focus specifically on the more problematic aspects of their role.

The size and complexity of the professional tutor's task means that the design of appropriate courses will certainly not be easy. Maw (1975) has suggested that the training of tutors in the school sector should incorporate three main elements: the knowledge and skills needed for objective self-analysis; the knowledge of group dynamics and the ability to apply these in concrete situations; and the ability to analyse their institution in terms of structure, communication, roles and norms and to convey this analysis to others in an acceptable manner. Our own findings would confirm the importance of these elements, together with specific training inputs relating to the disparate tasks itemized earlier in this chapter as currently being performed by professional tutors. Training courses will, then, need to be broad in scope and of an essentially multi-disciplinary nature, and will represent a lengthy and demanding process. Ideally it would seem that at least part of the training process should occur prior to an appointment being taken up. The diversity of experience and qualifications possessed by current and potential tutors will undoubtedly pose problems for course designers. These could, however, be alleviated to some degree by courses which are modular in structure.

This raises the further question of who should provide
the necessary training. As the colleges of education
(technical) have been directed by the ACSTT Subcommittee
to investigate the training needs of professional tutors,
it may perhaps be assumed that they will also be called
upon to act as providers. If this is indeed the case,
the question must be asked whether these establishments
currently have the range of expertise which will be required to mount such complex schemes of training.

Before leaving this subject, it is important to note that
there is no clear agreement within the FE sector as a
whole regarding the kinds of qualifications and experience that professional tutors should be required to
possess. When principals in our study were questioned
on this, few were able to offer concrete suggestions.
There was some feeling that an M.Ed. would be useful and
that the tutor should have previous experience of working
in an FE college. In general, however, the main factor
taken into consideration when making a professional tutor
appointment was that of personality, with particular
emphasis being placed on tact and diplomacy. There is,
then, little recognition of the importance of systematic
training.

Overview

It is apparent that general confusion abounds regarding
the role of professional tutors and staff development
officers. Without doubt there is a need for clarifi-
cation of the terms applied to those involved with staff
development. Unless a commonly shared terminology exists,
issues in the area of role definition will be obscured.
Such organizations as the Southern Network, the National
Association for Staff Development and the Association of
Professional Tutors might collaborate to produce guidelines in this area, leading perhaps to a national agreement on the terms and their usage. The APT has already
been engaged in preparing a code of ethics and professional conduct.

Both internal and external factors were seen to influence
the staff development positions created in a college.
It need hardly be stressed that considerable variation
existed regarding the type of appointments made. Our
study would indicate that an even greater variety of
arrangements may be found in the future. For example,
one college reported a proposed scheme whereby one professional tutor would serve all six colleges in their

county.

Although it is argued that counselling and responsibility for the professional education of teachers are integral elements of the role of a head of department only a small minority of teachers maintained that they had approached, or been approached by, their heads regarding their teaching skills or development needs. It should be recognised, however, that the personnel aspect of a head's job has become increasingly difficult as departments have grown in size and problems with accommodation have resulted in departmental teaching being carried out on more than one site. It is less common today to find the cosy departmental atmosphere in which a head can maintain a paternalistic interest in his staff. This is not to say that heads of department do not have a significant part to play in staff development. As has been pointed out elsewhere, 'staff development is an integral part of any department and the creation of external staff development roles in the college does not remove the obligation from the HOD to identify and establish the types of staff development exercise that are required in the department. Some of these may not need external help or resources' (Davies and Taussik, 1980, p15).

As the overwhelming majority of staff did not consider that a vice-principal could fulfil the duties advocated for a professional tutor it would seem that if both the vice-principal and the tutor are to be involved with staff development the areas in which each will work will need to be closely delineated. It is in any case essential for a tutor's duties to be clearly specified and generally agreed upon. From our own responses to questionnaires, interviews with FE staff, discussions with professional tutors and analysis of published material we are led to conclude that a professional tutor should:
- implement a college's staff development policy;
- devise and organize a basic introduction course for all new staff joining the college;
- play an important part in the induction process
- provide support for new entrants to FE, in particular for new untrained teachers;
- liaise with teacher training institutions and where requested, supervise trainee teachers undertaking teaching practice;
- initiate and assist with curriculum development;
- act as a counsellor for staff;
- be responsible for maintaining an up-to-date directory of courses currently available and provide for the dissemination of this material this can take the form of a regular circular to staff;

- advise staff on applications for attendances at courses, including applications for LEA financial assistance and possibly undertake some of the administrative work involved;
- organize in-service courses and seminars on teaching methods, audio-visual aids, administration etc, and be available to offer advice on these matters;
- participate in the teaching of educational subjects.

The items listed above may be seen to be those duties which it is expected that all professional tutors, by virtue of their status, should perform. Broadly speaking, both tutors and staff in this study regarded them as fundamental elements of the role.

He or she may also:
- assume responsibility for the compilation and updating of the college handbook;
- supervise the mentor system in a college;
- co-ordinate arrangements for research and consultancy, industrial and commercial secondments, and any teacher-exchange scheme.

It would appear that there are few objections to professional tutors' fulfilling these duties. However, there is strong disagreement regarding whether or not it is appropriate for a professional tutor to:
- be involved in the selection of new staff, including attendance at selection boards;
- assist in any appraisal scheme;
- be involved in decisions relating to promotion;
- monitor the classroom performance of teaching staff, including the observation of teaching.

Tutors participating in our study clearly recognized the potential for conflict inherent in these areas.

It was noted that, in order to perform this demanding role, professional tutors will need to undergo a systematic training process which must be expected to beebroad in scope and of an essentially multi-disciplinary nature.

Finally, we anticipate that for some years to come professional tutors will continue to construct their role. Colleges are still far from achieving an overall consensus in this area, as is evidenced by the remark made by one of the tutors in our study: 'I am now being pulled apart by the principal and vice-principal who are beginning to see my role differently'.

CHAPTER 6

Induction

Programmes which introduce newly-appointed staff to an
organization, prepare them for their responsibilities,
and generally give support and advice are common to many
professions. In the past further education colleges have
often relied on the goodwill of experienced colleagues
to provide the necessary help and support new staff
require. However, the growth and increasing complexity
of FE institutions have meant that formal schemes are
now becoming more prevalent.

The term induction has been the cause of some confusion
within FE and many colleges have used it to describe
what others would refer to as 'introduction'. Introductory courses are far more common than induction
courses. They last from half a day to a week, usually
before the start of the Autumn term or in the administration week. A typical introduction to a college
familiarizes new staff with the work and general running
of the college, introduces key personnel, and outlines
the role of bodies such as the RAC, the LEA and NATFHE.
In most respects an introductory course is peculiar to
an individual college. The term induction is generally
used in a much broader sense to include the whole process by which a new member of staff settles down in a
college and becomes confident in his or her teaching.
It can be argued that the induction process should begin
when a post falls vacant in a college. How the job
specification is drawn up, the nature of details sent to
candidates, the interview procedure, and the steps taken
to ensure that the successful applicant is given access
to college facilities prior to official arrival, are all
part of induction. An induction course during the
first year of appointment might attempt either to supplement teacher training and deal with practical problems
new staff encounter or, for untrained entrants, to

provide some pedagogical training as well. Existing
courses vary in length from a single week to one session
a week for the first term or for the whole of the first
year of appointment. It is to the availability of this
type of course, rather than the introductory courses,
that increasing attention is being paid.

The proposals for induction outlined by ACSTT (1975)
reflected the wide range of experience and training of
new entrants to FE, and were designed to ensure that 'all
teachers in FE have at least the minimum professional
teacher training necessary to equip them for their task'
(p5). The first recommendation was that 'not later than
1981 there should be a training requirement for all new
entrants to full-time teaching in FE who have less than
three years full-time equivalent teaching experience'
(p19). For those without pre-service training or equivalent, the proposed induction scheme was intended to
fulfil the recommendation of minimum training. It was
suggested that such staff should teach for three-quarters
of a full-time teacher's normal contact hours, and be released to train for at least one day a week for a year
with periods of block release. For new lecturers, who
had already completed a pre-service course it was proposed
that training should be limited to one day a week for
one term. The main emphasis in induction arrangements
for the untrained should be 'practical rather than theoretical' and 'should take account of differing needs of
those teaching mainly advanced courses and those teaching mainly non-advanced' (p9). In addition it was recommended that all new staff, whatever their previous
training or experience, should have an introduction to
their role in their new institution.

The RAC responses to Circular 11/77 outlined both current
provision for teacher training, including induction, and
proposals for future changes to meet the ACSTT proposals.
They suggested that the majority of colleges do operate
some form of short introduction to the college for new
members. However, provision for the induction of new
staff exhibited wide variation both within and between
RACs. Several of the submissions cast doubt on the
practicality of the ACSTT recommendations in the current
economic climate; in some colleges the small intake of
new untrained teachers and the variety of vocational
subjects taught made provision of a college-based
induction course difficult. Many of the reports suggested that at present their recommendations could only be
regarded as long-term objectives, though all agreed that
the first priority must be to ensure that all colleges
run a course to introduce new staff to the college. The

second priority was to be the provision of an induction course for untrained teachers with less than three years teaching experience.

Provision in the 19 colleges

At the time of our investigation only one of the colleges studied did not operate an introduction or induction course for new teachers, but was in the process of organizing one. Overall, however only 39 per cent of respondents to our questionnaire reported having attended an introduction or induction course while employed at their present college. Of these, the majority had attended courses of one or two days in length; the introduction of longer induction courses in recent years meant that a small number had attended courses lasting between one term and a year.

Colleges seldom make specific provision for staff who join during the course of the academic year, usually expecting them to attend an induction course at the start of the next year. This led to a frequent complaint that by the time teachers were able to take the course they had already found out the information by 'trial and error'. In an attempt to overcome this problem one college was investigating the possibility of video-taping induction sessions. On the other hand, there were those who felt that such training was in any case better left to the second year when new staff have had time to 'settle down'. Some colleges had already extended their introduction programmes along the lines ACSTT recommended, and one had successfully negotiated its induction as a valid entry to a second year 'certificate' course. Other variations in provision included a training programme run jointly by a number of local colleges. Here staff attend a short college-based introduction varying from one day to a week in length. Untrained lecturers then attend a common training course on one day a week plus two block periods. All staff new to ILEA colleges attend a similar course at Garnett College.

Views on introduction and induction courses

Short introductory courses were generally felt to be useful in helping new staff adapt to the college situation. The practice of holding them in administration or enrolment week was however criticised by many staff, including heads of department, who felt that new staff could benefit more from spending this time in the department. One suggestion was for these courses to be held prior to the start of the college year, though some teachers felt

that help and guidance was most needed, and problems
easier to recognise, once teaching had begun. Alternatively, it was proposed that an introduction should only
last a maximum of three days to allow staff more time to
get to know their department, courses and future students.
Any administrative or organizational details not covered
in the three days could be presented at a later date
when staff had had sufficient time to become knowledge-
able about the college. An outline of one college's
introduction scheme is reproduced as Item 6.1.

Item 6.1

Example of a college introduction course for
new full-time staff

Day 1

9.30	The present and future role of the college	Vice-principal

10.00   Tour of the college

10.45   Coffee

11.00	Staff organisations 1. The staff association 2. NATFHE	 Association Chairman NATFHE Branch Secretary

11.30	College administration	Chief Administration Officer

11.45	Staff development	Adviser for Staff Development

12.00	Audio-visual resources	A-V Aids Officer

Day 2

9.30	The development of the college	College lecturers

10.00	The library and the computer	Librarian and Computer Centre Manager

11.00	Welfare services	Senior Welfare Officer

11.15	Careers	Assistant Careers and Appointments Adviser

11.30	Open forum Questions answered by:	Vice-principal, Chief Administration Officer Adviser for Staff Development and three Heads of Department

Timing, length and immediate relevance all appear to be important considerations in running a successful introduction. It must avoid being too superficial and yet not swamp new staff with information and regulations. Teachers who had joined colleges before introductory courses were available felt that they would have benefited from such information, if only to avoid breaking 'unwritten' college rules. One method of reducing the length of an introduction course is to provide much of the information it covers in a handbook. Eight of the colleges in our study issue a handbook to all new teaching staff, but the majority of these are an addition to an introduction course, rather than a substitute. Sixteen of the nineteen colleges ran an induction programme varying in length from one or two hours a week for one term to a similar period for a year, sometimes including periods of block release. The longer induction courses were often run externally, linked to Cert.Ed. courses or the CGLI 730. Only ten colleges ran their own internal induction programme. In colleges with a full- or part-time professional tutor he or she is responsible for running the induction, and may also call on staff from other departments for help. In other colleges staff from the education department, who have responsibility for organizing CGLI teacher training, might also be involved. Outlines of two induction schemes are reproduced as Items 6.2 and 6.3.

The most frequently mentioned gain from an induction course was the opportunity it gave to meet staff from other departments. Many colleges, particularly those with split sites, appear to have very little communication and informal contact between departments. The absence of a common staff room and the sheer size of some institutions means that staff rarely meet colleagues outside their own discipline. Another favourable outcome was that staff become acquainted with the tutor running the course who, as already noted, would often be the professional tutor or a member of the education department. As a result, in contrast to more experienced staff who had not attended an induction course, they were better informed about staff development opportunities and were aware whom to contact concerning such activities.

Much of the criticism of induction programmes centred around their concentration on imparting information, rather than attempting to help new lecturers with more intangible teaching problems. In one college most staff who had attended an induction course for two terms were highly critical, both of the content of the programme and the methods employed by the staff teaching it. It was

Item 6.2

Induction into teaching - two terms (28 weeks) Fridays
1.30 to 4.30 pm

First Term

Week
1 a) Introduction to the course; information on course
     members
  b) Course planning: types of course
2   Schemes of work
3   Lesson plans
4   The student, the lecturer and the law
5   Personal relationships with staff and students
6 a) Class control
  b) Practice lesson by student (lecturer)
7   Assimilation and writing of reports; technique
     of quicker reading
8   Two practice lessons by students
9   Audio-visual aids. OHP - sound and video tape -
     films
10   Photography - slides
11   Chalkboard - Charts - Posters
12   Two practice lessons by students
13   Teaching methods - Lecture 1
14 a) Teaching methods - Lecture 2
   b) Practice lesson by student

Second Term

1 a) Teaching methods - Lecture 3
  b) Practice lesson by student
2   Student handouts
3 a) Examinations: GCE : RSA : C & G : Joint Committees
                                               etc
  b) Educational Technology
4 a) TEC - Structure
  b) TEC - Units
5 a) BEC - Structure
  b) BEC - Units
6   Assessment methods
7   - personal
8   - student
9
     CCTV
10
11   Staff Development opportunities
12   Review of the course

Note: Assignments will be given most weeks and records
       kept.

93

Item 6.3

Induction course for newly appointed staff, Autumn Term, Monday afternoons 3-5pm

Week

1 a) Geography of site - short tour
  b) Syllabuses, schemes of work and lesson plans

2   Visit to second college site and tour

3 a) Material resources, libraries, rooms, equipment
  b) Student counselling and welfare

4 a) College structure - an introduction
  b) Classroom techniques

5 a) Relationships with the environment
  b) Assessment

6 a) Staff development
  b) College management and committee structure

7 a) Finance I - estimates
  b) Audio visual aids I - reprography in the classroom

8 a) The future for Further and Higher Education
  b) Audio visual aids II - sound and picture in teaching

9 a) Audio visual aids III - TV as a teaching medium
  b) Finance II - resource allocation

10 a) Conditions of Service and Tenure of teachers
  b) Organizations and role of LEA

11 a) Safety in the college
  b) Examining bodies, validation of courses

12 a) Outside influences on the college
  b) To be arranged

13   Feedback session

commonly felt that the tutors tended to keep to a rigid work schedule and refused to try new approaches suggested by the staff attending. The tutors themselves felt that the whole exercise was very flexible and dictated by individual needs. Most specifications for induction courses indicated that the basic skills of teaching would in fact be covered, particularly for those with no experience or training, and in several colleges courses had been altered over the years to put more emphasis on the practical aspects of teaching - 'the nuts and bolts' - rather than on theory. Indeed induction courses are often regarded as a preparatory phase to further development, perhaps leading on to a full certificate of education taken the following year or soon after this.

One induction course that places particular emphasis on
supporting staff in tackling teaching problems is run on
a regional basis. During four consecutive days of enrolment week new staff without any formal training or
with little experience attend a residential course which
can count towards further teaching qualifications. As
well as an introduction to teaching skills and styles,
lesson preparation and presentation, each new teacher
records two short teaching experiences on video tape
for discussion and criticism. The tutors in charge of
the scheme suggest that 'students have always considered
the short teaching experiences to be the most valuable
aspects of the course. By providing two sessions, a
change of teaching style can be attempted.' Changes in
the course since its inception have included allocating
two tutors instead of one to review each teaching session filmed, in order to make criticism less subjective.
Only a very small number of staff in our investigation
had attended this course, but they were all compliment-
ary about it suggesting that it was 'invaluable to the
new teacher'.

The attitudes to induction courses of senior staff,
particularly heads of department, have a direct effect
on attendance. Despite a college recommendation that all
new staff should attend an introduction or induction
course, it is effectively up to each head of department
to ensure that staff are free at the appropriate times.
Many heads we spoke to suggested that, although they
were in favour of these courses, it was not always possible to release staff to attend, particularly in small
departments or where increasing demands were being made
by experienced staff for remission for curriculum development work, course attendance and special responsibilities.
Others are so keen to give staff every opportunity to
attend that they have been prepared to cancel classes to
do so.

As stated previously, the ACSTT proposals recommended
that new untrained staff should be given at least 25 per
cent reduction in class contact hours during their first
year, as well as release to attend an induction course.
One of the items in our initial questionnaire asked
staff who had entered FE teaching in the last five years
whether their teaching load had been reduced in this
way. Only 16 per cent said this had occurred, and the
reduction for the majority was one hour. A small number
of staff were given remission from teaching of up to
nine hours, but this sometimes included time spent

attending an induction programme. We investigated this point further in interviews with heads of department and recently appointed staff. As we suspected, the amount of remission granted varied considerably between departments and colleges: one college does not grant remission to staff for any purpose, while in a more typical college some departments grant two hours reduction per week to new lecturers while other departments make no such reduction.

The probationary year

In contrast to school teaching there is no statutory requirement for further education teachers to serve a probationary year, although local education authorities may operate such a scheme if they choose. Even in authorities where there is no policy of probation many FE colleges traditionally regard the first year of service as such, and in some cases make formal reports to the local authority. A formal probationary assessment usually requires that a new teacher is observed in the classroom by the head of department or professional tutor. When asked whether they formally observed teaching, most heads in our investigation said they or their senior departmental staff usually watched new inexperienced staff teach, although they rarely did so in the case of other staff. However, only a few of the colleges refer to the probationary year in their induction programme, or produce official assessment forms.

Opinions regarding the benefit of the probationary year varied widely. In one college a group of probationers who criticised their induction programme in a report to their college staff development committee made the following comment, which was reinforced by new staff in other colleges: 'The impression gained by most of the probationers was that classroom visits, on which it is assumed that much of the assessment is based, were simply to enable the assessor to write a report on the teacher visited. It was unusual for the teacher to have his shortcomings explained to him in any depth and to discuss how to improve his teaching'. In another college probationary teachers were kept better informed about their progress. Here the induction programme states that during the first year 'attendance and progress reports will be kept. In addition, arrangements will be made for the professional and staff tutors to sit in with new staff during their lessons. These visits will be followed up by tutorials and records will be kept. The head of department will be informed of the progress of new staff. Copies of these reports and the final course report will

96

be given to the students (lecturers) concerned'.

Making the process of probationer assessment more constructive from the new teacher's point of view would
seem to be a much needed and worthwhile move. New staff,
although in need of help in coping with college organization and administrative procedures, feel that induc-
tions generally fail to provide adequate support and
guidance to help them become better teachers. It seems
likely that staff would be more ready and willing to
accept criticism and help in terms of staff development
activities, if the basis for this is established in the
first year of teaching. To give the impression that a
teacher who manages to pass the probationary period is
'safe' from any further criticism ignores the way that
teaching skills develop and change to meet new
situations.

Support systems

The practice of formally assigning a new entrant to a
particular member of staff, who has overall responsibility for his or her well-being, has often been regarded as unnecessary in further education colleges. It is
assumed that most new staff will go to colleagues in
their section for help and advice, and that a formalized
'mentor' or 'sponsor' system is too rigid. Nevertheless
one of the recommendations of the ACSTT report (1975)
was that every new member of staff should be allocated
to a mentor, sponsor or 'colleague tutor' who is
'preferably of the same grade and sex and inhabits the
same staffroom' (p28). We therefore compared staff
views on the success of formal mentor systems, where
these were in operation, with those in colleges where
such relationships were left to chance.

Only six of the nineteen colleges we studied have a
formal mentor system. In the majority of the other
colleges an informal system operates - it is usually
left to individual departments to decide how new staff
are to be helped, and whether any one particular colleague
is singled out as an adviser. Even in colleges where
staff development policy and those in charge of staff
development activities claimed that a formal mentor
system operated, heads of department sometimes disagreed
as to whether the system was a formal one in practice.

The level of staff who take on the duties of mentor,
either officially or unofficially, varies considerably.
In some departments, particularly those with few staff,
the head of department or deputy head fulfils   this role;

97

in others, course or year tutors are presumed 'to have the welfare of their team at heart'. The professional tutor, members of an education department, or departmental staff development committee representatives are also regarded as appropriate mentors. The criteria used to choose mentors and the nature of their responsibilities are also regarded differently by different heads of department:

'Mentors are chosen on the basis of sex, age and specialism. Responsibilities are largely a function of the personalities involved. Minimum requirement is communication of college folk-lore, who's who, where to find it and how to get it, etc';

'... chosen so that their personality will complement that of the new member of staff, and also for their particular expertise and experience. They take part in the probationary assessments and generally encourage new teachers or those undertaking new subjects';

'Provision of syllabus, schemes of work - encouraging the new members of staff to involve him or herself in the development of work areas in which he or she shows most interest. Explaining the resources and facilities available to staff. Every month discussing the new staff with the head of department';

'I choose a colleague who is slightly older and more experienced (but not too much so) and who has, if possible, a similar subject area. Also I try to choose someone who has a good record for dealing with routine matters and lively approach to teaching.'

Personality obviously plays a major part in the success of any formal mentor system and it was suggested that it was difficult to find 'a compatible personality who will listen and help, but not dictate or interfere'. 'Age gaps' and 'differing ideas on how to deal with situations' were also considered to pose problems in choosing mentors. One head of department suggested that such problems militate against the introduction of a formal system, since one did not know the new member of staff until he or she had already settled in. Thus it was impossible to appoint an experienced teacher to act as a mentor in the knowledge that there would be no clash of personalities. Most heads of departments agreed that the mentor should be a specialist in the same discipline or, if possible, have experience of the course undertaken by the new members of staff.

The reaction of staff below head of department level to a formal mentor system was very divided. The majority felt that the system had both advantages and disadvantages; less than 4 per cent felt that it was without any snags

at all. Typical comments in colleges operating a formal
mentor system included: 'Those, like myself, who enter
teaching from industry with no training and no knowledge
of the way of life of an educational institution definitely
need a mentor';   'The mentor enables new teachers to
obtain help from a willing member of staff of sufficient
experience to know the problems that are likely to be
encountered in the first years of service';   'The mentor
helps you settle in quickly to a new environment at a
time when it is either sink or swim'.

Yet attention was drawn to the danger that, if mentors
were not chosen carefully, they might instill their own
prejudices into the newcomer, 'perpetuate old habits,
good and bad', 'possibly start you off too quickly in
bad ways', or 'even encourage a lack of self-reliance'.
As one lecturer commented: 'It is better to obtain help
and advice from the specialists involved than to rely on
one single person'.

Those favouring a more informal system commented that:
'It is no good appointing a mentor, suggestions can be
made, but a sympathetic colleague is always the best
mentor';   'the present ad hoc system means that the
person most competent to give advice on any topic will
usually give it'.

The view that 'some teachers prefer to find their own
way into college life' is valid, but a formal system does
have the virtue that staff who feel the need for guidance
can ask for help 'without the feeling of inconveniencing
someone'. Staff who had not been attached to a mentor
often referred to their reluctance to bother colleagues
with questions and problems when they joined the college,
since they felt either an extra burden to already busy
staff, or too embarrassed to admit ignorance. As one
teacher put it: 'A new member of staff always has a
number of small, rather unimportant questions which he
may be embarrassed to ask colleagues for fear of wasting
their time'. Provided mentors were given sufficient time
to carry out their duties, a formal system could remove
this reluctance. Few colleges do however give mentors
any remission from their teaching, and this perhaps explains the criticism of one new teacher that 'when one's
mentor was needed he/she would be teaching or otherwise
occupied'.

The direct involvement of mentors in the assessment of
probationary teachers was officially recognised in only
two of the colleges we investigated. In other colleges
the opinions of mentors are involved in deciding whether

a new entrant passes the probationary period, although
the principal of one college stressed that mentors who
are representatives on the staff development committee,
'make no report of any type on the new teacher's work'.
The direct involvement of mentors was particularly dis-
liked by new staff in one college who felt reluctant to
seek advice from a colleague who was bound to report on
their progress. As one teacher commented, 'the element
of assessment must be completely taken out and helpful-
ness emphasised'.

An archive system of teaching materials is a different
form of support found in a small number of colleges.
Materials are continually contributed by all teaching
staff to a central store and this is available to all
department staff. It can include syllabuses, teaching
aids, past examination papers and timetables and as one
head of department commented 'is a boon to the new
teacher'. In one Engineering Department senior staff
reported that such a system had been introduced some
years ago with the aim of encouraging staff to exchange
teaching responsibilities every few years. At first
teachers were said to object to having to give away their
work for others to use, but soon realized that they
benefited too. If any member of the department left the
college, the system enabled a new teacher to pick up the
threads very quickly. However, it appeared that once
the archive had been established it was gradually allowed to become out of date, as staff lost their initial
enthusiasm, and the original intention that it would
allow frequent changes in staff responsibilities was
forgotten. Nevertheless, such a system would appear to
have enormous benefits for new staff and it is to be
hoped that the practice will become more widespread and
popular.

Overview

In the current climate of financial constraints and
falling staff recruitment, the priority attached to
induction courses might appear questionable. Yet,
whatever their numbers, new teachers entering further
education colleges are still going to experience difficulties and may still continue to have no formal training. Even for trained entrants continual changes in the
skills demanded, due to the introduction of new curricula
and new groups of students, mean that these courses may
have to fill gaps in pre-service training and lay the
foundation for future in-service staff development.

None of the induction schemes we studied was regarded as

ideal by all staff. This is not to say that many staff did not find the schemes useful, but the diversity of backgrounds and expectations of new entrants to FE colleges means that any single course is unlikely to be seen as entirely satisfactory by all those attending it. As a survey of induction of new entrants to full-time teaching in further education colleges in the North-West concluded: 'It is impossible to recommend any single type of induction procedure which would be equally suitable for all colleges'. (NWRAC, 1970, p14). However, the comments of staff in our own study do suggest a number of improvements that could be made to current provision, and point out the disadvantages of certain approaches. For instance, it seems that most new staff benefit from a short introduction to college administrative procedures, personnel, formal and 'unwritten' regulations. Limiting the introduction to two or three days in administration or enrolment week appears to be the most popular approach, so that staff can get to know their own department at the same time. The provision of handbooks and possible meetings to discuss problems later in the first term or year is also recommended. Attaching new entrants to a mentor may have both advantages and disadvantages, but is generally regarded as a useful means of helping new recruits to settle quickly into a department.

Induction programmes must tackle some of the practical problems teachers are likely to encounter. A 'bird's eye view' of teaching theories, administrative procedures, audio-visual equipment and recent curriculum changes is a good basis for an induction, but comments from staff indicated that there should be more emphasis on teaching techniques appropriate to specialist teachers, coping with discipline problems, and some insight into counselling skills. A common criticism was that all theory on teaching assumes that students are motivated and self-disciplined. A small-scale study of recently appointed teachers at a number of further education colleges indicated that inexperienced staff were often 'anxious to achieve class control' and were 'sometimes afraid of disruptive students and apprehensive about actual hostility, as well as indifference'. (Harding et al, 1977, p227). Our evidence would support this finding.

CHAPTER 7

Initial teacher training

The emphasis placed in recent years on initial
pedagogic training is reflected in the priority many
colleges and local education authorities have given to
this activity, in terms of supporting applications for
release and providing financial assistance. One principal in our investigation cited only a single benefit
of his college's staff development programme: 'a very
large proportion of the teaching staff are now teacher-
trained and therefore up-to-date in modern methods and
techniques'. Although other principals would generally
list broader effects of their development schemes, the
majority nevertheless placed considerable emphasis on
the importance of increasing the number of lecturers
with a teaching qualification.

Current provision

The lack of any compulsion for teachers to train before
entry to FE has led to the development of a number of
different types of voluntary training provision varying
in length, mode of attendance and design. Full-time and
part-time courses are in the main provided in England
by the four former colleges of education (technical) –
Bolton, Garnett, Huddersfield and Wolverhampton – and
in Wales jointly by University College Cardiff and the
University of Wales Institute of Science and Technology.
Three main types of initial training are offered by most
of these institutions: a one-year full-time course
similar to the post-graduate certificate of education for
school teachers; a four-term sandwich course for
serving teachers, two terms of which are usually spent
at the training institution; and a two-year part-time
course which includes short periods of full-time attendance at the training institution. The limited number of
places at the main institutions, and the preference of
many colleges to train staff on a day-release basis has

meant that a network of extra-mural centres has been
established. These offer two-year day release courses
leading to a certificate in education with blocks spent
at the main institution. These outposts have become
increasingly popular as few colleges opt to second staff
for the in-service sandwich course, preferring a less disruptive pattern of secondment for perhaps one day a week
for two years, rather than for a full two terms. As a
result there are now more than thirty extra-mural centres
operating in different regions of the country. A small
number of University Departments of Education and Polytechnics also offer FE options on postgraduate
Certificate in Education courses.

Alternative teacher training is offered by the City &
Guilds of London Institute FE Teachers' Certificate
Course (CGLI 730). This is offered at some 170 colleges
throughout England and Wales, and although primarily
intended for part-time FE teachers, it has been taken by
full-time staff who wish to train, but who have been
unable to obtain release to a full certificate course.
In some colleges full-time teachers are encouraged to
take the CGLI 730 before taking the full Cert.Ed. The
Royal Society of Arts offers a Teachers' Certificate in
Office Arts and in the Teaching of English as a Foreign
Language. These courses are also aimed at part-time
staff, but over the years have become popular with some
full-time staff teaching in these subject areas. It
should be noted that neither the CGLI nor the RSA courses
lead to a 'recognised' teaching qualification; staff
who possess these certificates must complete a full
certificate course to gain this status. The College of
Preceptors also operates a training programme for
Associateship and Licentiateship which is recognised as
degree equivalent.

Dissatisfaction with this somewhat *ad hoc* system has
led to demands for a rationalization of FE teacher
training. The ACSTT Report (1975) recommended that 'there
should be an appropriate body in each region (either an
institution or, more probably, an inter-institutional
committee), to secure the co-ordination of arrangements
for validation' (p11) and a national forum 'for consultation between those concerned, with a view to ensuring
comparability of standards in courses and full transfer-
ability' (p11). To date, however, there have been no
moves to implement these recommendations on a national
scale.

The emphasis placed on initial training was evident in
all the colleges we visited. Many could point to

dramatic increases in the total number of trained staff
in the past few years due to a policy of in-service
training and the recruitment of trained teachers. In
some colleges there was a marked difference in this
respect between departments. Principals and staff
responsible for teacher training and development often
remarked that Catering and Building department staff
were invariably the keenest to train, while staff teaching in departments with a large proportion of advanced
level work were less eager. The ACSTT proposals to train
all new entrants to FE may in time balance these disparities, although it is unlikely that untrained staff
who feel they have been teaching successfully for some
years will see the need to pursue this type of development. Indeed some experienced teachers deliberately
avoid pedagogic training as the following remark by a
senior lecturer illustrates: 'I got wind of the fact
that it might be suggested to me that I take a Cert.Ed.
course. I didn't feel the need for this as I have no
problems with my teaching, so I took the opportunity to
take an MSc rather earlier than I had planned'.

College policy on training staff who have long teaching
service varies considerably. Some principals and heads
of department claimed that all staff regardless of age
and experience are encouraged to take a teaching qualification; others felt that alternative development
activities are more suitable. Ensuring that all new
untrained teachers are released to train may, however,
mean their more experienced colleagues have to wait
before being granted release, unless they too decide to
take a Cert.Ed. As one principal commented, staff in
his college are aware that 'there is no point in applying
for remission or funding for other development as any
allowances that are available have to go to teacher
training'.

Teachers' reactions to initial training

Of the staff below head of department grade who responded
to our questionnaire, 65 per cent had or were completing
the CGLI 730 course. Each of the colleges we studied
tended to favour a particular mode of training: two are
themselves outposts of a college of education (technical),
three send staff to local polytechnics to follow CNAA
certificate courses, while the majority send staff to
train at the colleges of education (technical), their
outposts or the universities in Wales.

In this section, teachers' views on Certificate in
Education courses and on the City & Guilds Teachers'

Certificate will be considered separately, although
similar comments were made about aspects of both types
of initial training.

Certificate of Education

We began by asking teachers to state the basis on which
they had undertaken their study while at their present
college. Their responses for Certificate in Education
courses are given in table 7.1.

Table 7.1   Types of release granted for Cert.Ed. courses

	Completed at present college	Currently studying	Total	
	%	%	%	N
No release	8	7	8	24
Day-release	32	40	34	103
Full-time secondment	11	6	10	31
Remitted hours	13	22	15	46
FE leave*	2	1	2	6
Block/sandwich	29	22	27	4
Not applicable/ No response	4	1	4	12
Total %	100	100	100	306
N	234	72	306	

* Note: FE 'leave' is a term commonly used to describe
        a method of release whereby a teacher's class
        contact is concentrated to allow a free half or
        whole day to attend a course.

The move away from sandwich courses and full-time secondment and the increase in the number of lecturers given
day release is evident from a comparison of those studying for a certificate at the time of the research with
the number who had already completed their training.
The change to day-release initial training is generally
due to college or local authority policy, rather than to
teachers' personal preference. Only occasionally did
teachers report having asked their college for permission
to follow a particular training course which differed
from the one the college usually encouraged staff to
attend. The influence of financial considerations was
evident; several staff we interviewed suggested that
because of pooling arrangements they were unable to
obtain release to attend locally-run training courses,
and instead were forced to travel outside the area. In
certain authorities day-release courses are favoured
since it is often easier to finance cover for staff
absences of one day a week than for a term or a year,

though in some cases it was reported that authorities provided no finance for covering staff.

Staff who had attended a Cert.Ed. course since joining their present college were asked if they would recommend this course to others. Their responses suggested that no one mode of attendance was preferred by a majority of teachers in comparison with other modes. The lack of consensus evident in questionnaire responses was confirmed during interviews with staff at all levels. For every teacher who stated a preference for a particular mode of attendance there was generally one who condemned it. Staff who had attended on a day-release basis were, however, generally more critical than those who were given block release or secondment. Typically it was felt that this mode of attendance was extremely hard to combine successfully with teaching commitments. As one teacher commented: 'Although the day release for the Cert.Ed. was sufficient in total time, I would much prefer to remove myself, say, a term at a time on the old block method. But this leaves no-one to run my course. A sabbatical term would be excellent but one can understand the staffing difficulties and the disruption this causes students.'

The majority of colleges reported that they grant remission for training, varying in length from two to four hours a week. Teachers often suggested that, in practice covering for staff absences and the difficulty of replacing a specialist teacher meant that they often 'lost' this remitted time. Others complained that, to be able to attend a course for half or a whole day a week, their classes were concentrated into four days, so that they still had to prepare for the same number of classes, as well as complete course work. Remission of a couple of hours was commonly said to 'just vanish' amongst administration and teaching commitments. In two colleges no remission was available.

Most colleges now try to encourage staff to commence a training course within the first few years of teaching, and all the colleges in our study release new untrained staff for teacher-training 'as soon as possible'. In colleges where there are sufficient resources to allow new entrants immediate release there is some disagreement as to whether training is best commenced in the first or second year of service. In six colleges it is college, or local authority, policy to release all new entrants to attend a certificate course in their first year, but in two others this release is deliberately given in the second year, since it is felt that in-service training is too great an extra load for first year teachers. This decision seems justified in the light of teachers' comments that they could rarely give sufficient attention to the course, when so many immediate problems faced them in the classroom. However, the recommendation in the ACSTT Report (1975) concerning the introduction of college-based induction courses for all new staff in their first year may mean that more colleges have no alternative but to insist that new entrants begin a course immediately.

Staff differed in their views regarding the relative merits of pre- and in-service training. For staff entering teaching after a period of working in industry it was felt that pre-service training offered a relatively painless introduction to the FE system. In contrast there was an equal number of teachers who felt that only with practical experience of teaching could real benefit be gained from training. A third view was that training was of little value in comparison with experience in 'the school of hard knocks'.

Table 7.2 shows the responses of teachers to a questionnaire item asking about the overall benefit of a Cert.Ed. course to their teaching. The largest number of teachers felt that the course they had followed was generally beneficial, although a small proportion felt that there are both advantages and disadvantages to training.

Table 7.2   Perceived effects of a Cert.Ed. course on teaching

	Completed before entry to present college %	In-service at present college %	Currently studying %	Total %	N
of benefit to teaching	63	60	26	60	473
of no benefit to teaching	10	13	5	11	85
both positive & negative effects	8	11	2	8	64
no response	19	16	39	21	169
Total %	100	100	100	100	791
N	485	234	72	791	

The most common opinion stated on the questionnaire and in interviews was that teaching practice was without doubt the most useful part of the course, while the theoretical component was less important. This might be expected of inexperienced teachers attending a pre-service course, since teaching practice provides an opportunity to experiment in a 'sheltered' teaching situation. Typical comments of such teachers were that 'training gave a good basis for lesson preparation, syllabus contents and broadens your outlook before any involvement'; 'It definitely helped me get a job, but any benefit was derived solely from teaching practice'; 'The chief value gained from periods of teaching practice and observation. More observation periods would have been beneficial'. However, more experienced staff also shared the view that the courses often seemed unrelated to practical teaching and the majority felt that they could be made much more practical. Heads of department often criticised the relevance of much of what their staff were taught on training courses and the absence of instruction on how to motivate difficult students. Although most continued to support college policies of priority given to such training, they made no secret of their personal reservations.

Teachers of social science and economics were particularly likely to be critical of the course they had attended, often feeling that the sociological, psychological and philosophical elements were too simplistic and 'inappropriate for people who have degrees in humanities'. Lecturers with no previous experience of these subjects frequently found this side of the course more satisfying and a number commented how helpful the psychology they had studied had been in understanding their students' behaviour. Yet the experience of one member of an engineering department provides an illustration of the danger inherent in a course offered to staff with varied backgrounds. This man was, in the words of his head of department, 'a superb craftsman' who had been forced to withdraw from a training course, since its content, especially the theoretical aspect, was pitched too high for his capabilities. As a result the teacher concerned had lost morale - in the head of department's opinion, unnecessarily. This would seem to indicate the need for training courses of different kinds to cater for the very different needs of FE staff. Although many courses do try to separate teachers of different subject specialisms, teachers participating in our study suggested that this does not always prove possible in practice.

In addition to the benefits of teaching practice, another frequently cited benefit of a certificate course was the

introduction it gives to the use of audio-visual aids.
One teacher summed up his course thus: 'It had too
little practice, inapplicable tuition and a lack of
academic work, but I make a classy visual aid'. Other
teachers saw the acquisition of these skills in a more
positive light, although lack of facilities in their own
colleges was frequently blamed for subsequent absence of
audio-visual aids in their teaching. Apart from these
reactions to specific aspects of their training, a small
number of teachers pointed out that their reaction to
the course as a whole had changed in retrospect. Their
initial response had been that the course was a waste of
time, but as one teacher said she now feels that she
'got something out of it and perhaps unconsciously applied
the things I learned'.

Experience in schools, whether as a qualified teacher or
on teaching practice, was often seen as being very
important when working with recent school leavers, since
it provides a clear idea of students' previous experience.
Several teachers in departments dealing with YOP and UVP
courses had such experience, and had found it was particularly valuable in this type of work. Certainly the
ACSTT Report recognised the overlap between the two
sectors: 'Some staff teaching the 15-19 age group need
to have an understanding of both further education
institutions and secondary schools (including Sixth
Form Colleges); and that there is a need to develop
better communication between the two sectors. We therefore recommend that consideration should be given to the
possibility of further education teachers, and indeed
some prospective school teachers, undertaking teaching
practice in both sectors during their training'. (ACSTT,
1975, p6)

One of the most frequently made criticisms of the current
training system concerned the high pass rate; we heard
of numerous occasions when teachers who were said to be
experiencing teaching difficulties were sent on a training course with no improvement in their performance on
their return, but with a teaching certificate. Many
heads of department expressed disappointment that training institutions allowed teachers to gain qualified status
when they were unsuited to teaching. Often training
institutions respond to such criticisms with the defence
that it is not their responsibility to do the colleges'
'dirty work' by failing teachers whom the college does
not have the courage to dismiss for teaching incompetence.
A vicious circle has thus developed, because it can
equally well be argued that before a college can dismiss
a teacher, it is bound by law to do everything possible

109

to help that teacher improve.

The whole topic of teaching incompetence is surrounded
by controversy and much of the difficulty college manage-
ments experience in dismissing teaching staff is due to
the social stigma attached to failure in teaching. The
view that 'anyone can teach' is still widely held at
least outside the profession and by ignoring pedagogic
training in the past, FE has helped to keep it alive.
Until it is accepted that failure at teaching is not a
handicap to other employment, colleges and teachers will
be loathe to tackle the subject of incompetence. In
the meantime the high pass rate merely serves to lower
the qualification in many teachers' eyes and deters some
from training.

The views of college staff about the tutors at external
training institutions were obviously influenced by individual personalities and whether or not the approaches
adopted were seen as suitable for their own needs. However a criticism that was made by slightly more than half
of those who had taken a Cert.Ed. course was that the
tutors appeared to have become 'out of touch' with classroom practice, and were often unfamiliar with non-advanced
work and the teaching techniques appropriate to it.
Training institution staff would undoubtedly dispute this
accusation, on the grounds that their staff either have
recent FE teaching experience or maintain close contacts
with local colleges. One head of department who was a
former member of one of the colleges of education
(technical) asserted that such criticism, although perhaps justifiable in the past, was currently unfair, since
these colleges now made an effort to recruit staff with
recent teaching experience. Others argued that staff
reports of their training suggested that the courses
were of little help in solving their classroom problems,
and as one head remarked, 'if one of them (a college of
education (technical) tutor) had to teach my students
they would eat him'.

A solution to the apparent isolation of teacher-trainers
which was frequently put forward was that they should
either share their service between colleges of education
and FE colleges, or be seconded to full-time teaching
for periods throughout their careers. This is by no
means a new idea - several university education departments already carry out such schemes and in a recent
experiment in Wiltshire a school teacher and a teacher-
trainer at the University of Bath exchanged jobs for
half the week for a year (Lodge, 1980).

A further criticism of teacher-trainers is that they rarely 'practice what they preach', and thus do not serve as a useful model. The need for teacher-training to be self-demonstrating and for tutors to have up-to-date experience of the work for which they train was in fact emphasized in the 1978 ACSTT Report. Although this Report covered the training of adult education and part-time FE teachers such requirements surely apply to any teacher-training.

Not all the teachers in our sample would support these criticisms of tutors on training courses; though it must be said that those who could not fault their trainers were far outnumbered by teachers who could suggest improvements in their performance and approach. One comment made by a teacher who had been seconded to train for a year was that it was refreshing to be treated as colleagues rather than students. Other typical comments of this nature included: 'A well organized course. Good tutorial support when needed.' 'Advice from tutors on assessment led to improved presentation and variation in teaching methods.'

Expectations and past educational experience influence such reactions and, as in all colleges, there will be good and bad teachers in training institutions. Yet it seems that more teacher-trainers will have to be seen to have recent contact with current teaching, and practice the techniques they teach before the notion that 'those who cannot teach, teach teachers' is totally forgotten in FE. The question of who trains the trainers is one that has remained in the background for many years, but deserves more consideration in the light of the emphasis now being placed on pedagogic training for further education staff.

City & Guilds 730 teachers' certificate

Many of the views on Certificate in Education courses were echoed by staff when considering the CGLI 730 course. Since this is taken on a part-time basis, usually for one or two evenings over a period of either one or two years, comments concerning the benefits and disadvantages of this mode of attendance resembled those made about day-release Certificate courses. Thus the difficulty of combining a training course with full-time teaching commitments was repeatedly mentioned. Similarly, a local or in-house course, with little disruption to family commitments, was regarded as being more attractive than taking a full Certificate course at a college of education (technical). Eight of the nineteen colleges in fact

111

run their own CGLI 730 course. In contrast to full
Certificate in Education courses the CGLI 730 was slightly
less often criticised as lacking relevance to teaching
(see Table 7.3), and it was suggested that the course was
flexible enough to be geared to individual needs and
successfully to combine theory and practical teaching
advice. Thus typical comments on the benefit of the
course to teaching included: 'a sound grounding on the
study and preparation of material for teaching purposes';
'helped with planning of lessons - how to set out and
time lessons and schemes of work'; 'gave a broader outlook on teaching'.

Table 7.3   Perceived effects of a CGLI 730 course
on teaching

	Completed before entry to college %	Completed at present college %	Currently studying %	Total %	N
Of benefit to teaching	55	65	25	58	76
Of no benefit to teaching	7	11	–	8	11
Both positive & negative effects	4	3	–	3	4
No response	34	21	75	30	39
Total %	100	100	100	100	130
N	56	66	8	130	

Overall, 70 per cent of teachers who had taken, or were
taking, the CGLI 730 course reported that they would
recommend it to their colleagues. This was particularly
the case among staff with practical backgrounds or
limited experience of FE.

Fifty-three per cent of the teachers who answered
questionnaires and had or were taking, the CGLI 730
had taught part-time before their first full-time appointment. Many had taken the qualification when they were
still teaching part-time. It is said by senior staff in
FE that part-time teachers are particularly keen to
develop themselves in comparison with their full-time
colleagues. One possible explanation of this tendency
is the isolation of part-time teachers, who are often
present in colleges only for their teaching duties.

Thus staff development activities provide a welcome
opportunity to meet colleagues and discuss their teaching. This could partly explain the surprising number of
part-time teachers who are prepared to train in their own
time without the remission that applies, at least in
theory, to full-time staff. However, the favourable
opinion of the course held by the majority of teachers
with no part-time experience belies any suggestion that
this satisfaction is related solely to part-time status.

The lack of qualified status on completion of the City &
Guilds Certificate course and the need to take a full
Certificate to obtain this qualification resulted in frequent complaints from teachers. Those who had taken a
Certificate course after the CGLI 730 complained, almost
without exception, that they found the second course
repetitious and in some cases inferior. It seems that
a move to establish the CGLI 730 course as the first
year of a full certificate course, or allow teachers
exemption for this qualification, would be widely appreciated by teachers who feel the repetition wastes both
their time and limited staff development resources.

As in the case of Cert.Ed. courses, it was commonly
stated that the tutors were often guilty of not practising the style of teaching they advocated. Yet there was
some feeling that, as in all courses, benefit to an
individual often depended more on the calibre and
commitment of other teachers in a given year group, than
on the curriculum or course tutors. A minority had
reservations about the course as a whole, and felt that
a full teaching certificate was preferable and better
suited to FE teachers' needs.

Overview

Teacher training, although no longer the only major form
of staff development in FE, still dominates the policy
and practice of many local authorities and colleges.
Despite recent efforts to recruit trained entrants to
colleges and to increase the number of places for staff
to train on an in-service basis, it will be some time
before the majority of FE teachers are trained to teach.
Incentives or pressures to train are unlikely to do much
to change the attitudes of a number of experienced staff
who feel that training is irrelevant to their particular
situation, and even changes in the nature of courses
may do little to alter such ingrained attitudes. Nevertheless our investigation does suggest that there is
room for some restructuring of training courses. Although
the views of teachers in our study concerning their

training were as diverse as the courses they followed, there was consensus on a number of issues; changes in the emphasis, mode of attendance and content of training courses were advocated by a significant proportion of teachers, particularly in relation to the Cert.Ed.

It appears that individual staff members will always favour particular modes of attendance at initial training courses. Ideally, lecturers would like to be able to choose the mode of training which suits their own circumstances, rather than follow the course preferred by their particular college or authority. It therefore seems sensible for the current range of training modes to remain and for teachers to be allowed greater freedom of choice. Financial restrictions may encourage more local education authorities and colleges to favour day-release attendance over secondment or sandwich courses. Such a move to increase day-release provision for certificate courses is not likely to be popular if it is not accompanied by realistic release from class contact, particularly in the case of new teachers.

The present financial climate means that many teachers have to wait some years before they are released to train, by which time training often appears less relevant. Priority for release for training is usually given to new untrained staff, but the policy of releasing teachers in their first year to pursue external training courses was felt by some staff to be adding unnecessarily to teachers' workloads. The ACSTT proposals for induction courses for all newly appointed staff in their first year of appointment, leading for some to a second year of study for full professional status, assume that new teachers will be given adequate remission and lightened timetables. The findings outlined in the previous chapter indicate that this does not always occur. Similarly, for external teacher training courses, lecturers often complained that remission was not given or was inadequate.

Overall, some 60 per cent of our questionnaire respondents regarded their classroom practice as having benefited from the training course they had attended. In the case of pre-service courses or those taken in the first years of employment, most benefit was felt to derive from teaching practice which allowed staff to 'find their feet' without a great deal of pressure. For more experienced teachers, practical sessions were again felt to be of most use, and many lecturers appreciated the chance to step back from day-to-day teaching and reconsider their work.

The common complaint that discussion of teaching difficulties was hampered by the range of subject expertise
of teachers attending both college-run and external training courses points to the need to try to cater for
specialist teachers. Ideally, previous qualifications
and educational experience could also be taken into account
when the grouping of teachers is considered. Obviously,
the limited numbers of teachers at any course prohibits
such fine distinctions. Yet without more specialized
provision many teachers will continue to feel training
courses are too generalized and cannot possibly be related to the current changes that are affecting their
particular discipline. Concern about specialized provision is connected with the view of many teachers that
tutors on training courses appear to be somewhat out of
touch with current developments in FE. Tutors must
demonstrate that they do have continual contact with
'front line teaching', and also exhibit in their own
teaching some of the techniques they advocate. The training and development of teacher trainers needs continued
review and as new institutions such as polytechnics and
universities enter the FE training field, consideration
must be given to ensuring that their staff understand
the workings of FE. Teachers generally favoured the
idea of tutors sharing their employment between FE
colleges and colleges of education, or at least being
seconded to FE teaching at frequent intervals in their
careers.

The high pass rate for training courses also requires
some attention. It may be a genuine indication of the
proficiency of the majority of FE teachers, but is more
often regarded with suspicion, and jeopardizes the
seriousness with which training is viewed. Finally, one
of the most pressing concerns is the integration of the
many different types and levels of teacher training. The
implementation of the ACSTT proposals on induction and
training may lead to a rationalization of initial training. But financial restrictions and the absence of any
co-ordinating body may delay this. FE teachers would
certainly welcome a unified system so that exemptions
for example for those with City & Guilds Certificates,
would prevent what is regarded as wasteful repetition on
full certificate courses.

CHAPTER 8

Post-experience training

In a rapidly changing society, few would dispute that FE staff should undertake training throughout their working lives. Staff need to keep abreast of developments in their subject specialisms; in technological, industrial and commercial practice; in education and teaching techniques. Clearly the diversity of staff employed in the FE sector calls for a wide range of approaches, from attendance at short courses and registration for further and higher qualifications to regular spells in industry and commerce, and research in a specialized area. For individual teachers, moreover, training will have to be appropriate to different stages in their careers.

While these needs were acknowledged by both the James and Haycocks Committees, recent financial constraints have meant that resources are not available to support all teachers in updating and extending their experience and qualifications. Although the ACSTT Report (1975) recommended that release for in-service training should be five per cent of the FE teaching force at any one time, DES Circular 11/77 suggested that three per cent might be a more realistic target. Many LEAs now doubt, given the current financial situation, that even this figure is feasible and are at present actually reducing in-service training budgets.

External provision

Ironically, cutbacks in budgets are occurring at a time when recognition of the need for FE staff to refresh their experience and gain new subject knowledge or pedagogical skills is greater than ever. The 1978 annual conference of NATFHE, for example, passed a resolution instructing the National Executive Committee to prepare a detailed claim to secure for teachers an entitlement to sabbatical leave. We found considerable support for

this measure and often staff themselves admitted that
after a number of years teaching they had become 'stale'.
Even though a wide variety of long courses are available,
it is often the cost and, concomitantly, the possibility
of remission and/or study leave which determines not only
whether teachers will take up opportunities but also the
actual choice of programme.

In only four of the study colleges was it likely that
staff might obtain a one-year full-time secondment for
further in-service training. For the academic year
1979/80 a total of 22 secondments were made by these
colleges. Of the other 15 institutions, no secondments
at all had been granted in eight, and in the remaining
seven it was said either that secondments were rarely
granted or that they were limited to one or two annually;
these were usually allocated either to teachers who had
to be redeployed or to those taking or completing a
Certificate in Education.

Remission for part-time study for long courses was awarded by 12 of the 19 colleges. In the remaining seven
where no reduction in class-contact hours was possible
(except for induction and initial teacher-training),
efforts were made to accommodate staff members wishing to
pursue further qualifications by rearranging timetables.
Provision for remission varied widely among the 12 colleges - ranging from one to six per cent of total class-
contact hours. It should be borne in mind, however,
that not all of the hours remitted were necessarily
available for staff development purposes. Although
some colleges indicated that the demand for remission
was increasing, all reported reductions in recent years
in the total number of hours available.

Staff who had studied for further qualifications were
of the opinion that remission was highly desirable, if
not essential, for the successful completion of a course.
In interviews a number of teachers stated that they had had
to withdraw from a study programme because the pressures
of work proved to be too great. It was a source of grievance to some teachers that although their college granted
remission for external long courses this was not awarded
if similar study was undertaken at the college itself.

Staff seconded for full-time courses have their registration and tuition fees met in full and invariably travel
and other expenses are also refunded by the LEA. Financial provision for those attending part-time study varies
with the nature of the course (DES Circular 14/70:
Administrative Memo 26/70). Courses that can be claimed

back from the pool were said in the majority of colleges
to be 'almost automatically financed'. In all colleges
application procedures for full-time secondment and remission were broadly similar. Staff were expected
initially to complete an application form and most commonly this was provided by the local authority. Some
colleges, however, had devised their own forms on which
staff were usually expected to provide details of their
teaching career to date; present qualifications; previous in-service training; details of the proposed
course; estimates of costs involved; and reasons for
their application. A separate section of the form had
then to be completed by the applicant's head of department, who was expected to indicate whether or not the
application was supported. In some colleges heads were
also required to describe the arrangements which would be
needed to cover the teacher's absence. While in 14
colleges applications were then forwarded directly to
the vice-principal or principal, in five these were first
presented to the staff development committee.

In most colleges successful applications for secondment
and part-time long courses had to be formally approved
by the Academic Board before they were forwarded to the
College Board of Governors and LEA. Most education
authorities required that an applicant should have had
at least five years service with the authority prior to
a secondment being awarded and it was commonly stated
that requests to undertake teacher training would receive
priority over other forms of development. In addition,
one stated that it placed an upper age limit (45 years)
on candidates for secondment. LEAs differed in the
manner in which applications were processed. Whereas
in one, all college principals (or vice-principals) met
and decided among themselves the distribution of the
authority's total allocation of secondments, in others
principals reported that they were not consulted on the
matter. There was a widespread feeling among all study-
college principals that applications were being more
frequently rejected by the LEA than had been the case in
the past.

Staff were most dissatisfied with college application
methods where decisions regarding support were made by
one person rather than a committee and where criteria
for support (and priority listing) were unpublished.
The main criticism made by both heads of department and
teachers in these colleges was that decisions appeared to
be arbitrary and this was said to create resentment among
those who were unsuccessful. It was stressed that the
allocation of study awards and remission must be seen to

be fair. In the other colleges, while little objection
was voiced by teachers to the actual procedures, some
criticisms were made of the fact that secondments and/or
remission were less likely to be granted to a teacher
from a department which had in the past had a generous
allowance, and that specialist teachers from small
sections were at a disadvantage because they would be
difficult to replace.

The range and number of short courses has increased
dramatically in the past ten years. While the DES continues to be the principal organiser of in-service short
courses, other agencies such as universities, local
education authorities and the Regional Advisory Councils
are extending their short course provision. Many private
companies, especially in the electronics field, are also
mounting courses and conferences relevant to FE teachers
on an unprecedented scale. Indeed the majority of staff
believed that external short-course provision was more
than adequate, but that staff were not able to exploit
existing opportunities fully because the finance for fees
and release was not available.

In general, release for short courses and conferences was
said to produce fewer problems than that for long courses
as the former tended to be held during vacations and weekends. Considerable variation was nevertheless found
between colleges in the extent to which the expenses of
staff attending short courses and conferences could be
met. Fifteen had their own short-course   budget and,
with two exceptions, the sum allocated on an annual basis
by the LEA. There were however, significant differences
in the size of college budgets. Where colleges had no
budget, LEAs usually refunded applicants according to the
duration and nature of the course. It was general policy
that where a member of staff attended a course at the
instigation of the college full expenses would be reimbursed. In some colleges it was reported that the LEA
stipulates that only one course or conference may be
attended per year and/or financial assistance should not
exceed a stipulated amount. Both regulations were found
to be a source of grievance to FE staff who pointed out
that they could not afford to attend courses and conferences because of the financial expenditure involved.
Several heads of department stated that they had noticed
a sharp decline in applications since staff were expected
to bear an ever-increasing proportion of course costs.

Short course applications, after approval at the department level, were forwarded in the majority of colleges
directly to the vice-principal. There were two notable

exceptions: in the case of one college, heads of departments could authorize expenditure (having their own departmental short-course budget); in another, only the professional tutor's approval was necessary with regard to financial expenditure, although applicants had to have their absence (where appropriate) sanctioned by the head of department. In the latter case only unusual or expensive applications had to be referred to the vice-principal. Where applications had first to be approved by the LEA two main criticisms were made by staff: that applications had to be submitted too far in advance; and that formal approval generally took too long.

A wide variety of long and short courses had been attended by staff in the study colleges. One of the main reasons given for attendance was that of wanting to extend or up-date subject knowledge. Of teachers who reported that this was the major motivation, those who had first qualified a number of years ago considered that developments in their own subjects were so far-reaching that these could not be adequately covered by a three- to five-day course and a long programme of studies was deemed necessary. Without doubt, these teachers felt that their own teaching had improved and students had benefited as a result of their experiences.

Twenty-two per cent of teachers who responded to the questionnaire (excluding those who had studied for a Certificate in Education or the CGLI 730) had acquired further qualifications during the period spent at their present college. While one, eight and seven per cent of respondents had obtained Ph.D., Master's and first degrees respectively, six per cent had achieved professional and technical qualifications. It should be borne in mind, however, that these figures include both those who may have spent the whole of their teaching career in their present college and those finally completing qualifications for which the major portion of the work had been undertaken prior to appointment. Regardless of the type of long course undertaken the overwhelming majority of teachers stated that it was difficult to combine studying with teaching commitments.

The overwhelming majority of teachers interviewed believed that both they and the college had gained as a consequence of their studies. As noted earlier, teachers thought that students benefited from courses reflecting new developments. In addition a number of teachers pointed out that they thought it was to the college's advantage to have a more highly qualified and up-to-date teaching force. Those who had taken higher degrees also drew attention to the fact that their colleges were now able to run courses which they might not otherwise have been able to mount. Commonly, members of staff said that as a result of their studies they had a renewed interest in their subject and felt that this enthusiasm was conveyed to students and helped to produce more stimulating teaching sessions. One-third also believed that their career prospects may have been improved.

In all but two study colleges, staff were required to report back on courses attended; and in one college, fees are not reimbursed unless a report is submitted. Sixty-nine per cent of questionnaire respondents, however, reported that their college or department had no formal procedures. This discrepancy cannot be wholly accounted for by the likelihood that non-course attenders were ignorant of the procedures involved. The fact that in the majority of colleges reports had to be made to heads of department may also need to be taken into account, since we found wide variation in the methods used and the extent to which this requirement was enforced – even within the same college. While some heads expected written statements from teachers, others said that verbal accounts were acceptable and still others that they left staff members to decide whether or not it was worth writing a report.

As might be expected, methods were the most formal and standardized where reports had to be submitted either to the principal or staff development committee and in four colleges forms had been drawn up for this purpose. The most comprehensive of these is reproduced as Item 8.1. In this college it was stated that the object of the report was to ensure that staff derive the maximum benefit from the course attended and that limited funds are used wisely. The professional tutor stated that he keeps 'a close record of those reports which recommend that more staff should attend'. Copies of all forms are filed for general reference in the education section and all members of the academic staff have access to this information. Similarly, in a number of other colleges reports were intended to be of help to other staff when deciding on course attendance.

Item 8.1
A course attendance report form

Organising body

Address   Telephone

Duration   Dates

Frequency   One only   Mode   Day
            Repeated irregularly   Evening
            Repeated regularly   Residential

Location

Costs   Course   Subsistence   Travel
          fee
                      Accommodation   Additional

Additional relevant information
(eg attendance restrictions

ANALYSIS
OF COURSE

1 Give a synopsis of the course objectives

Were they: Satisfactory?   Capable of improvement?
Any comments:

2 Give a synopsis of the course content

Was the   Of great   Of some   Of questionable
content   relevance?   use?   value?

Did it   Successfully?   Adequately?   Poorly?
meet the
objectives
Any comments

3 Were appropriate methods used?   Yes   No
  Was the teaching   Good?   Adequate?   In-
  performance   differ-
                                          ent?

Please amplify any adverse comments

1 What is your overall   Very good   Reasonable   Poor
  opinion of the course?
  Any comments

2 Should any other individuals or groups   Yes   No
  of people be encouraged to go?
  If 'yes' please amplify

3 Are there any aspects worthy of wider   Yes   No
  distribution within the College?
  If 'yes' please amplify

4 Could we run similar courses for our   Yes   No
  own staff or for external people?
  If 'yes' please amplify

ADDITIONAL ITEMS
OF VALUE

Please give full details of any additional items of
value - eg:
1 Any useful contacts
2 Any valuable sources of information or reference
   material
3 Any schemes or ideas, possibly from other establishments, which might interest someone in the College

---

CIRCULATION

Please include anyone likely to benefit - not just
managerial staff
Staff Development Sub Committee
Teaching Development Unit

plus:

SIGNATURE   DATE

Staff members might also provide a short verbal report at departmental staff meetings. Less frequently, it was said that staff might give a lecture or seminar or arrange a workshop. In interviews teachers said that this rarely occurred but pointed out that they often learned informally about the content of courses and conferences. While many senior staff thought that at the present time insufficient effort was made to inform staff of their colleagues' training experiences some were not convinced that this was a practical possibility outside individual departments.

Internal provision

Six of the study colleges had attempted in recent years to mount an annual programme of in-house short courses. In these colleges six to ten courses, on average (organized by the education division or professional tutor) would be offered to staff. The courses were usually arranged on the basis of one-hour sessions per week and tended to last for five to six weeks. The programme given as Item 8.2, the most comprehensive we encountered, indicates the nature of provision. This was drawn up after a survey of the needs of the staff and in two other colleges programmes had similarly been devised in response to internal investigations. In a further five colleges short courses were run on an *ad hoc* basis and, with one exception where courses were provided by a joint consortium of colleges, two or three short courses, lasting one or two days were offered at the end of the academic year in the remaining colleges.

In those colleges without an annual programme, senior staff frequently stated that they would like to see more internal course provision. Indeed in several of these institutions steps were being taken to make such arrangements. In the majority of cases it was said that this interest in in-house courses arose from the present financial restrictions on spending, which would mean that fewer members of staff would be able to attend external courses. Some heads of department and vice-principals also drew attention to the high costs of travel and/or accommodation and therefore argued that internal courses 'make sound economic sense'. A minority of senior staff were also critical of past and present reliance on external courses and were of the opinion that in any event colleges ought to be running their own training programmes. The view was put forward that the college was in the best possible position to evaluate its own staff needs and courses could then be geared specifically to those. It was also pointed out that a college was

EDUCATION AND RESOURCES DIVISION
STAFF DEVELOPMENT SHORT COURSE PROGRAMME FOR FULL-TIME AND PART TIME MEMBERS OF STAFF

The programme offered below contains a number of short courses. Careful account has been taken of the response made by staff to the recent survey carried out. Please indicate the courses you are interested in attending on the attached pro-forma and return it to your Head of Department. Most courses will take place between 0900 and 1000 hours. On those occasions when the principal wishes to speak to staff at these times his meetings will take precedence. Fridays have been kept free for Academic Board and other meetings.

AUTUMN TERM

A. PROJECTS AND ASSIGNMENTS COURSE 1. 5 x 1 hour meetings. A course designed to familiarise teachers with the requirements of projects and assignment methods. Particularly useful for teachers of TEC and BEC courses.

B. TUTORIAL SKILLS COURSE 1. 6 x 1 hour meetings. This course will cover the basic teaching, counselling, social and administrative skills required of a tutor.

C. MULTIPLE-CHOICE TESTING COURSE 1. 5 x 1 hour meetings. An introduction to the uses and construction of multiple-choice tests.

D. TYPEWRITING - A SKILL FOR TEACHERS. 12 x 1 hour meetings. An introductory course for staff who wish to learn typewriting.

E. FIRST AID 1. 8 x 1 hour meetings. An introduction course to some basic first-aid techniques

F. AUDIO VISUAL AIDS WORKSHOPS 1. Practical s essions in which staff can make their own audio-visual aids with help from the Resources Section Staff.
1. O.H.P. Transparency production
2. Tape-slide production
3. Photography
4. C.C.T.V. and making simple T.V. films.

G. TEACHING REMEDIAL ENGLISH IN FURTHER EDUCATION

H. INTRODUCTION TO THE TEACHING OF THE HANDICAPPED IN FURTHER EDUCATION.

I. INTRODUCTION TO COMPUTERS

J. TRADEC PRINCIPLES. 3 x 1 hour meetings. Unified
Vocational Preparation schemes are being promoted
nationally in an attempt to extend the provi sion made in
in colleges to young people and jobs and industries
not traditionally associated with Further Education.
This course considers one approach to course design.

K. PROJECTS AND ASSIGNMENTS COURSE 2. 5 x 1 hour meetings.

L. TUTORIAL SKILLS COURSE 2. 6 x 1 hour meetings.

M. MULTIPLE CHOICE TESTING COURSE 2. 5 x 1 hour meetings.

N. TYPEWRITERS - A SKILL FOR TEACHERS (continued).

O. AUDIO VISUAL AIDS WORKSHOPS 2.

    1. O.H.P. transparency production
    2. Tape-slide production
    3. Photography
    4. C.C.T.V. and making simple T.V. films

P. FIRST AID 2. 10 x 1 hour meetings.

Q. INTRODUCTION TO COMPUTING 2.

    Course 1. 10 x 1 hour meetings

    Course 2. 10 x 1 hour meetings

R. TRADEC PRINCIPLES. 3 x 1 hour meetings

SUMMER TERM

AUDIO-VISUAL AIDS WORKSHOPS

    1. O.H.P. transparency production
    2. Tape-slide production
    3. Photography
    4. C.C.T.V. and making simple T.V. films.

FORM OF APPLICATION

Please tick the courses which you would like to attend
and return this form to your Head of Department.

    NAME

    Department

capable of responding quickly to emerging needs whereas it inevitably took time for an outside body to make suitable provision. In this context, reference was made in particular to the time-delay in courses mounted to prepare teachers for developments associated with TEC, BEC, UVP and YOP work.

It was, in general, considered essential that courses take place during the working day as staff were reluctant to take on extra commitments in the evening. In those colleges where sessions had been run at such times low attendance figures were said to have led to courses being abandoned. Overall, it was reported that internal short courses were poorly supported within the college and this also applied to long courses run internally, such as CGLI 731, 732 and 733. Organizers did not believe that this was solely accounted for by timetabling problems; rather they saw it as reflecting staff apathy. The number of staff attending each course was said seldom to exceed ten and we heard it stated repeatedly that it was 'always the same people who came forward'. Generally those courses which were reported as being most popular were on audio-visual aids, first aid and safety, and student counselling. Residential courses in those three colleges where these had been arranged, were well attended and spoken highly of by teachers. However, in two cases these are not likely to be repeated in the future because of the high cost of the enterprise.

When we sought teachers' own views on in-house provision, many said that they preferred to attend courses organized externally as these afforded the opportunity to meet colleagues from other colleges and provided 'a break' from their working environment. Clearly some teachers were reluctant to attend in-house courses because they felt that the college lacked the necessary expertise. In particular staff did not believe that specialist subject courses could be provided by the college itself.

At the departmental level few lecturers in any of the study colleges reported that meetings were held which enabled common problems to be discussed, experiences to be shared and information and new knowledge to be ex-changed. Very rarely indeed was it said that departmental seminars or workshops took place. Yet, as one recently appointed head pointed out, such meetings could afford an excellent opportunity for 'self help' and can be a means whereby teachers offer each other mutual support. While some teachers queried the need for such formal arrangements, stating that they already had informal discussions with colleagues on teaching-related issues,

127

others responded favourably. Some of these staff stressed that, should such provision be made, it was important
that meetings were well organized, that they did not
'degenerate into general moan sessions' and that they were
not attended solely by 'the young and enthusiastic'.

The suggestion was also proposed by a few senior staff
members that, since it would be impossible for courses
and workshops to cover all subjects and staff to attend
all sessions, information sheets on specific topics
should be produced. In one college a member of the education and resources division had produced handouts on
audio-visual-aids and in another a tape on behavioural
objectives had been made and was available to staff.
Mention also needs to be made here of the work of the
Council for Educational Technology. At the time of our
investigation only a fraction of the teachers in the
case-study colleges were aware of the packages produced
by the Council. It appeared to be the case in some
colleges that although the principal held materials
published by CET, the college had yet to develop the
means for its internal circulation.

Research

One of the first staff development documents to draw
attention to the role of research in college programmes
was the ACFHE/APTI Report (1973). Since its publication
there would appear to have been an increased awareness
of the desirability of staff undertaking such an activity,
even in colleges where little or no advanced work is
taught. Undoubtedly the growth of CNAA courses in FE
colleges has provided an impetus for staff to be encouraged
to develop research interests. Indeed in colleges with
a high proportion of advanced work we found that specific
reference tended to be made in policy statements to
research activities and that details were provided of the
criteria and procedures employed with regard to applications for remission for this purpose, (See Item 8.3).

Procedures for applications for remission and/or finance
were in all colleges (where these were formalized)
similar to those required for long part-time study. In
three colleges separate research committees had been
established and in these cases applications were submitted to them directly. In one college the committee
administered a small research expenses fund. While this
was the only institution where such an arrangement was
found, in another some finance was on occasions made
available by the college and in a further case it was
proposed that the LEA or other bodies be approached for

COLLEGE A

In evaluating projects for which support is requested the
Research Committee have to consider widely different
types of activity. The following criteria have been
adopted, though not all are necessary or sufficient to
gain support:

a) appropriateness to the development of the member of
   staff as a teacher in further and higher education;

b) relevance to the current or future teaching activities
   of the college;

c) enhancement of the general reputation of the college;

d) good quality;

e) group projects with some guarantee of continuity will
   be favourably considered;

f) the clear prospect of an end result; for example,
   a higher degree, design or publication;

g) value to industry or other appropriate outside
   organisation will be a recommendation.

Initial applications are made through the head of section
and head of department, who should agree to any remission,
to the Research Committee.

COLLEGE B

Consequently, applications for the commencement of a
research project should:

(i)   show evidence of preliminary investigation/study
        sufficient to indicate that the project will be
        practicable within the resources likely to be
        available;

(ii)   state the objectives of the research and an estimate
        of the time (academic years) which is likely to be
        needed to achieve the objectives;

(iii)   demonstrate that the project will relate to the
        teaching programme of the college or to student
        experimental work.

(iv)   confirm that a suitably experienced 'supervisor'
        has agreed to provide general support/guidance on
        technical matters within the chosen field.

(v)   indicate from the nature of the proposals the extent
        to which papers on the matters dealt with in the
        research will be available annually for internal or
        external publication.

funding minor projects up to £150. Although in half of
the study colleges formal provision and mechanisms
existed for supporting research, the staff themselves
frequently stated that it was extremely difficult to
obtain remission for research which did not lead to a
higher degree. Responses received in our interviews and
questionnaires indicated that a very small number of
teachers were in fact undertaking research that was not
linked to a qualification.

Overview

Attendance at long and short courses may perform a
variety of functions both for the individual and the
college. Two of the most significant aspects of this
form of development are that teachers' subject knowledge
may be up-dated or extended and that staff may find a
renewed interest in their teaching. As Watkins has
observed 'The mere avoidance of staleness is one of the
great justifications for in-service training' (1973 p14).
If mobility continues to be as restricted as it is at
present, the latter consideration may become of increasing importance. Moreover, as colleges appoint an ever-
decreasing proportion of young, recently qualified staff
there will be growing numbers of teachers who will need
to bring their subject knowledge up-to-date. It cannot
be hoped that this can be achieved solely by lecturers'
own private reading and attendance at short courses.

While many senior staff in the study colleges acknowledged
the need for post-experience training, few said that
they strongly recommended staff to enrol for long courses.
Indeed, teachers who had obtained qualifications while
at their present college commonly reported that these
had been taken on their own initiative. In a number of
cases it was stated that the impetus had been the reali-
zation that they were out of touch with developments in
their specialist area. Where secondments and reductions
in class-contact hours had been made, it was widely felt
that the attitude of the head of department towards staff
development, the priority which he or she attaches to it
and to particular types of course could significantly
influence the success or failure of a teacher's application. As in all but two colleges applicants for leave
and remission are required to obtain a recommendation
from their head of department, they may be regarded as
performing a gatekeeper role in so far as they can control
teacher access to resources.

The fact that a significant proportion of staff have been
prepared to take courses, despite in many cases teaching

full time-tables, and in some cases having to bear part
or all of the costs involved, must in no small measure
reflect teachers' enthusiasm and commitment to their
work. In eight colleges no secondments at all were
awarded and in seven no remission of class contact hours
could be made. While the majority of lecturers who had
attended long and short courses had received some
financial support it was widely anticipated that in the
future fewer would have all, or a portion of their fees
reimbursed. It was reported in some colleges that
teachers were already having to meet an ever-increasing
proportion of the cost of short-course participation.

If as predicted, remission and study leave become even
more difficult to obtain, it will be increasingly
important that staff consider that these are equitably
distributed both inside individual colleges and among
FE institutions in general. It would seem essential
that criteria for support are made known by the LEA and
the college. Teachers are less likely to feel resentful
where criteria are well publicized and decisions do not
appear to have been reached arbitrarily. With limited
funds available there is a special need for these to be
employed in such a manner that staff derive maximum
benefit. Basic measures which might be taken would be
to ensure that information on courses is efficiently
and promptly disseminated within the college and to
establish or review formal mechanisms by which staff
report report back on courses they have attended.
Regarding the former we found that in colleges without
a professional tutor it was often the case that staff
neither received details of short courses early enough
to permit attendance nor were sufficiently well-informed
about the longer programmes available. A regular
bulletin would be helpful in this respect.

In only a few study colleges was reporting back on
courses and conferences carried out systematically.
Indeed, in the majority of cases, it appeared that
although staff were expected to submit reports, this
requirement was not generally enforced. Report forms
provide a valuable opportunity not only to discover
how far staff felt their own requirements were met but
may also help in evaluating different types of programme
offered at local, regional and national levels. Not
only may this knowledge be of use in advising staff on
training courses, but also in influencing the direction
of resources towards those programmes which are perceived to be of greatest benefit. As Taylor (1977)
has pointed out we have at present few systematic
evaluations of in-service programmes and, as provison has

greatly increased in recent years, the quality of some may be doubtful. Additionally, much may be gained by making formal arrangements, where appropriate, for staff who have attended courses to inform their colleagues of any newly acquired knowledge, skills, or techniques: workshops and seminars in particular might be arranged. We found considerable variation between colleges and departments regarding the extent to which staff were required to provide such feedback, but it was apparent that in general colleges have yet to fully exploit this opportunity for development.

It was evident that all nineteen colleges relied heavily on external courses provision, though there were some indications that, because of current economic stringencies, greater attention was being paid to how in-house programmes might meet staff training requirements. Nevertheless, our findings suggest that it will be some time before college-focused in-service training is widespread. Internal short-course provision tended to be spasmodic and sketchy and, overall, both long and short courses were poorly supported by staff. Comments made by teachers especially regarding the credibility of their colleagues as tutors, suggests that it may be difficult to convince some that the necessary expertise exists to mount short-course programmes. This would appear to highlight the need for senior staff to give careful consideration to the selection and training of organizers and tutors. There may be advantages in inviting outside specialists to one or two sessions - this might also help to prevent courses becoming too inward-looking.

A further means by which development could be provided inside colleges is by encouraging staff to engage in research. It may be expected that even in colleges where non-advanced work is predominantly taught, there will be some staff for whom this may be the most appropriate form of development. It should be remembered that NATFHE considers 'there should be no arbitrary terminal point for the availability of research opportunities, whether in institutional terms or according to level of work; and that opportunities should not be restricted according to the type of institution' (Waitt, 1980, p744). Nevertheless, we found that those teachers pursuing research activities were largely confined to the colleges with higher proportions of advanced-level teaching.

CHAPTER 9

Industrial liaison

One of the major roles of further education colleges
is to provide vocational education; for this, lecturers
need to be conversant with current industrial practice
and the ACFHE/APTI Document (1973) drew attention to
the need for liaison with industry to be regarded as
fundamental to any college scheme. The ACSTT report
(1975) also recommended that since 'much of the work in
the colleges must be closely relevant to that of the
areas of employment to which their students go... there
should be more opportunities for teachers to spend
periods of secondment in the appropriate sectors of
industry, commerce or the public service' (p12). Similarly, in the education service generally the need to establish strong links with industry has been increasingly
advocated in recent years.

None of the RACs reported any formal policy on industrial
liaison for FE staff, although the Yorkshire and Humberside Council for FE indicated that a scheme to allow
teachers of distribution subjects to gain work experience
was being prepared. The Welsh Joint Education Committee
suggested that the CBI had initiated discussion with LEAs
about implementing the 'Understanding British Industry'
(UBI) scheme, though this may be intended primarily for
school teachers. Although industrial liaison is mentioned in a few of the staff development policies we studied,
it usually was said to be given lower priority than other
development activities.

In comparison with the schools sector, formal schemes to
encourage the secondment of FE lecturers to industry are
few. Perhaps it is assumed that day-to-day contacts ensure that lecturers can make their own arrangements - an
assumption that will be discussed further in this chapter.
Schemes that are in existence may be limited to a particular geographical area. The Southern Science and Tech-

nology Forum, for instance, is a body working in education and industry in Hampshire, the Isle of Wight and
Dorset, which encourages exchange of information and co-
operation between the two sectors. Teachers have spent
short periods in local firms during the summer vacation
under the aegis of this forum, but it appears that most
of the effort has so far centred on the school sector.

One scheme that is designed specifically for FE is administered by the DES. This scheme offers a limited number
of six-week placements in industry for teachers of chem-
istry, chemical engineering, mathematics, physics, bio-
logy and pharmacy. It is recommended that applicants
should normally be involved with classes at HNC level or
above, and preference is given to those with little or no
industrial experience. Each year principals of all major
FE establishments are contacted and asked to nominate
members of staff to take part. The decision to grant
paid leave of absence rests with each LEA. Although the
firms involved bear the cost of lodging and some travelling costs, it is suggested that LEAs try to provide sufficient expenses to allow lecturers to return home for
perhaps two weekends during the six week secondment.
Successful applicants are asked to submit a general
report of their activities first to the firm and then,
with their approval, to the DES. There are no equivalent
schemes for lecturers teaching other subjects and at
lower levels, although some industrial training boards do
offer short courses to update knowledge of industrial
practice.

Day to day contact with industry

When asked about the extent of their contact with industry
or commerce, many lecturers suggested that this was neither
as frequent nor as extensive as they would like. Of the
staff below head of departmentllevel who responded to the
questionnaire, 46 per cent said they had either no or
limited contact. It might be expected that these teachers
would come largely from departments where such contact was
less appropriate. However, 40 per cent of respondents
in departments of business studies, catering, construction,
engineering and science said that the chief method used
to keep in touch with commercial practice was through day-
release students. A small minority of lecturers felt that
this was sufficient, but the majority felt that student
contact could never be adequate to keep abreast of new
techniques and developments. For this, firsth and knowledge and experience was necessary.

Of the lecturers who said they maintained direct contact
with industry, the most common methods included visiting

firms to see students in placements or to recruit new
students; running courses on employers' premises; liaising with personal friends and former colleagues; or serving on committees with industrial representation. A
number of teachers, particularly in departments of catering and building, said they regularly worked in industry
during the vacations or sometimes at weekends. Only a
few lecturers reported having extensive contact with industry or commerce during term time. Generally such
teachers act as private consultants, carry out research
for local firms, run their own businesses, or teach courses
that involve considerable contact with employers.

Requests for closer and more regular contacts with industry
were not confined to departments specializing in courses
for industry. In particular staff in general studies
departments frequently suggested that they could benefit
from greater contact with the industries which employ
their students.

A minority of staff did feel the need for more regular
liaison with industry and commerce. This view is reflected in the following comment: 'Currently I have no
contact whatsoever with commerce; I don't feel that my
teaching suffers as I've had enough experience in life
and the low-level basics of commerce are still the same'.

Pressure of work and lack of remission to carry out
liaison work were most commonly given as reasons by
lecturers to explain their lack of regular contact.
Alternatively, in the catering industry, for instance,
the hours that employers work was said to prohibit contact during college hours. Even those lecturers who are
fortunate enough to have remission for this contact
suggested that it was impossible to arrange visits and
keep up to date with developments adequately. The
introduction of new curricula, although often intended
to increase co-operation between industry and colleges,
was said to decrease still further the amount of time
available for liaison. It was also claimed that fewer
lecturers now go to firms to enrol students and so the
opportunity this provides to build up personal contacts
was lost.

Secondment to industry and commerce

The difficulties involved in maintaining day-to-day
contact with industry prompted many teachers to suggest
that periods of industrial secondment should become
common practice in further education. In the nineteen
colleges studied very few members of staff had ever been

seconded to industry or commerce. Of the questionnaire
respondents only three per cent said they had ever been
seconded for this reason, although two-thirds said they
would welcome such an opportunity. Interviews in the
colleges and senior staff questionnaire responses confirmed this. In every college the view was frequently
expressed - often by the principal - that industrial
secondment was a long neglected aspect of staff development, and that there was a growing need to update the
experience of technical teachers in current industrial
practices.

In one college a committee set up to consider staff
development matters had recommended that industrial
secondments should be encouraged and given priority
over other development activities. In a second college
the staff development panel was considering drawing up
a formal policy on the matter at the time of our investigation. A few lecturers had been seconded to industry for short periods in the past in this college,
and a discussion paper has been written to consider
the desirability of formalizing and expanding this
type of development. The panel asked heads of department by questionnaire about the means by which their
staff update their skills and knowledge of industry.
Four of the seven heads said one or two lecturers had
been seconded to local firms in the last few years ,
although the time-span varied from two weeks to one year.
In comparison with other colleges in the study, this
number of secondments was unusaally high, yet all the
heads felt that a formal secondment programme would be
a useful innovation. The discussion paper concluded
that a secondment programme would be difficult to
implement within the limited college budget, and would
be more likely to succeed if it were developed with the
support of the local authority. However, it was
suggested by the senior management, at a later visit to
the college, that current financial restraint would
probably mean that no action in this direction could
be considered for some time.

A small number of staff, although in favour of secondment,
suggested that the difficulties involved, including
covering the classes of the staff released and finding
employers willing to accept teachers at a sufficiently

high level of responsibility, would hamper any formal
scheme. As one head of engineering reported, 'many
employers are not prepared to give teachers the degree
of involvement necessary for real benefit to be gained
from the experience on a temporary basis'. After
several unsuccessful attempts to second members of his
staff he felt that consultancy was the only practical
way of maintaining industrial contact at present.
Similarly another head commented that 'industry finds
it very difficult to prepare and run a programme which
is both genuinely useful to the teacher and a meaning-
ful contribution to the firm by the teacher'. Other staff
also pointed out that in any secondment scheme it would
be important that lecturers had a 'real' job to do and
were not 'treated as passengers'. It was suggested that
this might mean lecturers had to undertake a period of
induction prior to the secondment.

There was some disagreement over the ideal period of a
secondment. Some felt that only when seconded for at
least a year could a member of staff really be 'absorbed'
into an organisation and so truly benefit from the experience. Others felt that much shorter periods of
release, perhaps at different stages in a lecturer's
career, would be more valuable. In both cases difficulties were envisaged; during a long-term secondment,
pension rights might not be safeguarded and replacement
staff would be difficult to find, while employers
might be reluctant to take on staff for very short
periods. Senior staff generally said it was easier to
arrange secondments on a one-day-a-week basis rather than
full-time, since covering for classes was much less
difficult.

Obtaining permission from a local education authority
for lecturers to return to industry was often cited as
a serious difficulty. One head of department commented
that LEAs often proved harder to convince of the value
of industrial interchange of staff than industry itself.
Another head argued that when local authorities refuse
to grant leave with salary, the reluctance of staff to
return to industry on periodic release was increased.
In other colleges it was common for any secondments to
be on the basis of unpaid leave. Staff were said to be
reluctant to accept this method, since there was some
anxiety that their posts might not be vacant on their
return or that their pension rights might be lost.
Senior staff suggested that one of the greatest deterr-
ents to industrial secondments was the fact that they
could not be charged to the 'pool'. In the words of one
principal: 'my biggest bugbear is the refusal of the DES

137

to allow periods of industrial placement to be charged
to the pool, thus effectively ensuring that we rely
entirely on approved award-bearing courses for full-time
secondment'.

The fact that the costs of industrial secondment are not
poolable and the limitation this places on the extent of
any arrangements was also mentioned in the questionnaire
response of one local education authority. This
authority is keen to encourage secondments of this sort
for teachers in all sectors of education, and it was
reported that three teachers, including one from further
education, were currently on one-year secondments to
industry. It was suggested that any request for unpaid
leave of absence from teachers wishing to improve their
industrial or commercial experience was looked upon
favourably. Most of the other authorities questioned
said they had no policy on industrial liaison, although
one did suggest that it was prepared to supplement the
normal secondment programme by releasing teachers for
appropriate industrial experience where 'suitable
arrangements can be made to cover the teaching commitment
and to offset any additional expenditure in the release'.

The feasibility of secondments was also said to depend
on the expertise of the staff member concerned. For
instance, the head of a construction department suggested
that it was easier for craft teachers than for 'profess-
ionals'; the former could be more easily taken on as
foremen, but employers might be reluctant to take on the
second group, as there would be no guarantee that they
would be able to see a project through in the time
allowed. In contrast, several teachers of management
and business studies suggested that it would be quite
feasible to exchange jobs with personnel officers,
training officers or trade union officials. Other
teachers raised the problem of their 'acceptability' to
employers. In one instance, a lecturer in nursing
studies reported that his RAF training would not be recognised in a state hospital - yet hospital experience
would be valuable in advising students. Another suggested that employers were willing to take college staff
'only if they promised not to tamper with the machinery'.
Lecturers specializing in pure sciences pointed out that
it was increasingly difficult to arrange any type of
industrial placement since university and research establishments would generally only consider secondments
lasting two years, rather than the few months favoured
by colleges and LEAs.

An important consideration influencing a significant
number of teachers was the adverse effect secondment
might have on their students. The timing of short-term
secondments was felt to be very important since in an
examination term this could disadvantage students. An
interesting argument put forward by some lecturers was
the importance of staff being seconded to firms outside
the college catchment area to avoid loss of credibility
with employers and students. Lecturers espousing this
view expressed horror at the thought of working alongside
former students or, worse, under their control. In
contrast a small minority, said they would welcome the
opportunity to work in firms from which their students
came since 'it would be nice to see a friendly face'.

Staff in only two of the nineteen colleges reported
having taken part in the DES scheme to second lecturers
to industry and very few junior staff had ever heard of
it. In one of these colleges a lecturer, now a head of
department, had been seconded to ICI and had found the
experience enabled him to become familiar with new
instrumentation and techniques. Similarly two lecturers
in the second college had spent six weeks at another
ICI centre and they, too, had found this useful. None
of these staff said they had any difficulties in being
accepted by other employees or in arranging for their
classes to be covered in their absence. The firm's
section heads were said to have 'gone out of their way'
to introduce the college lecturers to other staff and
to their work, and one of the colleges even acquired a
piece of equipment which was no longer of use to the
firm as an added bonus. In one of the colleges taking
part in the DES scheme, lecturers in the biological
science department were keen to undertake similar short
secondments to update their knowledge of hospital
pathology practice. After lengthy discussions with
the local authority it was agreed to release two
lecturers each for six weeks. However, in contrast to
the DES scheme, no additional resources were given to
the college to cover for the staff absences. Lecturers
had to make their own arrangements with appropriate
organizations, but had not encountered any difficulties
in finding placements. Following the success of these
secondments, the college was negotiating with the local
education authority for sabbatical leave to be granted
annually for this purpose and for absent staff to be
replaced.

In other colleges, staff secondments to industry were
often said to be due to the efforts of individual
teachers or confined to a single department, perhaps

reflecting the importance attached to this activity by particular members of the senior staff. The head of one management studies department reported that an arrangement had been made with the local authority to allow lecturers to spend six weeks in its own management services department. This particular head recommended that there should be 'regular visits to appropriate industries together with secondment at, at least, five yearly intervals for periods of not less than one month'. A lecturer in another college took unpaid leave for two years to work in educational administration and management in the Far East, but his head of department reported that he had as yet had no suceess in gaining release for other staff to spend periods in local industry.

All other secondments were for much shorter periods. Two lecturers in different colleges had, for example, been seconded for one week to British Rail and British Gas respectively - the first as part of a local scheme of teacher secondment. Both had found the experience useful - as one commented it gave 'a valuable insight into how industry works and copes with training'. In other colleges a few lecturers reported spending one day or a few hours a week in local firms, perhaps to become familiar with new printing equipment or to gain membership of a professional institute. In some cases remission was granted for such visits, while in others lecturers reported that they undertook them when their workload allowed. Finding local employers willing to take staff for regular short-term periods of secondment was frequently said to be difficult - a typical comment was: 'Several firms were approached but were not working in the specialist field required and others could not fit one-day-per week working into their deadline structure'.

Overview

It is now widely recognised that teachers of vocational subjects need to be up to date in industrial and commercial practice, and thus able to meet the training needs of employers. It is also argued that even those lecturers who do not teach practical subjects would benefit from some knowledge of the type of work their students are likely to enter. Day-to-day contacts and consultancies have traditionally been regarded as an important way for lecturers to keep in contact with industrial practice. Yet our study suggests that the majority of lecturers feel that opportunities for liaison with industry and commerce are limited, and that there is a real need for colleges and LEAs to encourage and support such contacts. Two ways of improving the present level of liaison are by granting more remission for regular short-term contacts, and by making it easier for staff to be released for longer secondments. These suggestions are supported by other recent research studies. Thus during an investigation of curriculum development in FE colleges, it was reported that a large number of senior staff expressed 'a need for help in providing secondment and funds for more frequent "industrial-updating" of staff' (Russell, 1980, p211).

In our study the difficulties in arranging release for industrial and commercial liaison and secondment were frequently mentioned by lecturers at all levels. Problems in obtaining release from teaching duties for regular visits to local firms or combining this with a full timetable were commonly reported. Indeed only a small minority of lecturers said they had regular contact with local industry; most of those who did not suggested that this had a detrimental effect on their teaching. Similarly, finding suitable staff to take over classes or the finance to pay these staff was said to be the greatest obstacle to industrial secondment. Union opposition, especially in 'depressed' industries, and the reluctance of employers to give lecturers enough responsibility to benefit from a short spell in industry were also mentioned as discouraging factors. However such problems were not insurmountable, since some lecturers have managed either to maintain regular visits to local firms or, more rarely, to be seconded for periods of up to a year. In the case of day-to-day liaison this has generally only been possible because of personal contacts or business interests, or because of the willingness of some lecturers to use their free time and vacations. In the same way, secondments to industrial or commercial firms were often said to have been at the instigation of individual senior staff members or the lecturers themselves who, because of their belief in the value of this form of development, were not daunted by obstacles.

The ideal length of a secondment was a matter of some disagreement. Some staff favour a term, rather than shorter or longer periods, but few colleges have managed to release lecturers for this period. Others felt that regular shorter spells in industry would be more valuable in keeping staff conversant with new developments, and would enable classes to be covered more easily.

What can be done to help and encourage lecturers to keep up to date? As a first step the few existing opportunities to gain experience of industrial or commercial practice should be more widely publicized, since it appears that many lecturers are unaware that these exist. However, these formal schemes are still very limited, and some attempt must be made to make employers aware of the benefits of closer liaison. It seems likely that many employers have given little thought to the possibility of taking on lecturers or of their own staff spending periods in colleges to discover more about the education which employees receive. Firms already involved in liaison could also be encouraged to publicize their activities in the hope that this might persuade others to follow their example. If more organizations could be interested in taking part in the DES scheme, for instance, there might be less need for employers to pay lecturers' lodging costs, since secondments could be arranged locally.

Assuming that it will be some time before there are sufficient financial resources to allow a large expansion of provision for industrial secondment, alternative strategies for increasing contact might include joint appointments so that lecturers could work half the time in education, the other half in industry, commerce or the public service, or a growth in the number of projects which college departments carry out in association with industrial firms, thereby encouraging communication and mutual trust. Courses for lecturers and staff from local firms might be organized to promote more understanding, and dispel the ignorance of each sector concerning the aims and problems of the other. In two colleges it was reported that a lecturer was to be appointed in the near future to act as an 'Industrial Relations Officer' or an 'Industrial Tutor'. This person was to be responsible for creating and maintaining contacts with local firms – in one case for one department only (the Catering Department) and in the other for the whole college. It was anticipated that in both colleges remission would be given to an existing staff member to undertake these duties, and some staff questioned whether such a position would lead to increased liaison. However an appointment of this type, in demonstrating a commitment by senior staff to industrial liaison might encourage more lecturers to arrange visits or secondments.

CHAPTER 10

Overseas exchange

It is a long established practice for FE staff to participate in exchange schemes and undertake short visits
to other countries. In addition, some teachers have, on
their own initiative, spent periods of their career working overseas. Yet the ACFHE/APTI Report (1978) mentions
this aspect of staff development only once: 'Study leave
and study tours' (p12) features on a list of methods by
which development may be achieved, but is entirely absent
from the check list provided in the Report of items for
inclusion in a staff development programme. Only a very
small number of FE staff apply for exchanges or visits
organized through one of the official bodies with responsibilities in this sphere. Participation, it would
appear, tends to depend heavily on the individual's own
awareness of such opportunities and, although college
support may well be forthcoming, little initiative is
taken in actively promoting such activities.

Recognition of the potential of this strategy does seem
nevertheless to be increasing. The rising costs of
secondments and courses combined with the overall reduction of training budgets will mean that, if staff
development schemes are to be maintained, new and less
costly methods of development will have to be explored.
It may also be argued that as appointments become increasingly rare and promotion even rarer, so FE colleges
will be forced to consider means to minimise teacher dis-
affection, while at the same time generating fresh ideas
and approaches. A number of formal schemes already exist
for overseas exchanges, visits and placements, organized
by a variety of agencies, such as the Central Bureau for
the Exchange of Commonwealth Teachers, the Overseas
Development Agency and the Technical Education and Training Organization for Overseas Countries (now taken over
by Overseas Development Administration and the British
Council).

Participation in exchange schemes in the study colleges

Overseas exchanges and/or visits were referred to in the
staff development policy statement or other related
documents of only five of the study colleges. In one
college in particular procedures were well defined and
responsibilities in this area clearly delineated, as is
illustrated in Items 10.1 and 10.2. In the other four
colleges arrangements were less formalized and variation
existed regarding those staff who had major administrative
responsibilities in this area. In one college it is the
professional tutor, who undertakes much of the work related to exchanges while in another this job is undertaken by one of the four assistant principals. In the
latter case it should also be noted that the principal
actively seeks to establish links between the college
and educational establishments in other countries and
has been personally responsible for initiating a number
of exchanges.

Although the total number of staff who had participated
in a variety of exchanges and overseas placements was
small, it should be borne in mind this reflects the
current situation in which only a minute proportion of
FE staff avail themselves of such opportunities: during
the academic year 1979-80, only four teachers from the
FE sector participated in exchanges organized by the
CBEVE. The Central Bureau stated that this is not accounted for by the lack of suitable applicants but is indicative
of the low number of applications from FE.

We found that staff who had been on exchanges or who had
taken up overseas positions were drawn from a number of
subject specialisms and grades (from LI to SL). Their
ages spanned an unexpectedly wide range, 28 to 50, and
most had families who had accompanied them. In only
two cases were the members of staff concerned women. It
is of interest that most reported that the exchange was
not the result of long-term planning. Four teachers had
decided on 'the spur of the moment' to put in an application after hearing that they 'might have a chance'.
In general staff said that they had not taken the
initiative to discover the details of schemes; either
their heads of department or the principal had pointed
out to them that such arrangements existed. A variety
of reasons were given for having originally applied for
an exchange or overseas unilateral appointment. Most
commonly it was said that a change from college routine
was desired. Many of those who had been exchangees
stated that they saw this as an alternative to a move
to another college. Seldom was it considered that an
exchange had been undertaken for career reasons, although

144

Item 10.1

Teacher Exchange Arrangements

i) Administrative

a) The exchange of teachers between the College and colleges from other countries will be under the exchange
   arrangement organized by the Central Bureau for
   Educational Visits and Exchanges, the Department of
   Education and Science and the corresponding bodies in
   the other countries.

b) It is preferable that the exchange be in identical or
   or comparable fields of teaching, but it is not essential
   that it be so.

c) The exchange teacher will be required to un dertake
   a teaching programme agreed in advance with the Head
   of the 'host' department.

d) It is hoped that a one-to-one exchange of houses can
   be negotiated by the exchangees between themselves .
   The College cannot be a party in any such negotiations,
   nor accept any fina cial responsibility in respect of
   any contract agreed between the exchangees.

e) The travelling expenses and other supporting grants
   received by the UK exchangee, will be those applying
   at the time under the Department of Education and
   Science Teacher Exchange arrangements as administered
   by the Central Bureau for Educational Visits and Exchanges.

   All financial payments to the exchangee will be the
   responsibility of the sponsoring authorities, such as
   the Department of Education and Science. The College
   will not be concerned with any of these payments.

ii) Educational

a) Every opportunty and encouragement should be given
   to the exchange teacher to visit other institutions,
   organisations and places of interest which will enable
   him to gain the maximum benefit from his visits.

b) The aim of these visits could be to extend the exchangee's
   knowledge of his own specialization of interests, of
   the British educational system, the social and political
   systems, etc.

c) The teaching programme of the exchange teacher should
   be modified so that he can adjust to the new situation
   in the first place, and then benefit from the wealth
   of new experiences which are available to him.

d) The programme in the Autumn term should be lightened as a normal procedure for a new member of staff. After a normal teaching commitment in the Spring term of some 18 hours per week, the teaching load should again be lightened in the Summer term to allow for a programme of visits, carrying out a research programme, etc.

e) Where possible, a proportion of the exchangee's teaching time should be used in the College on the basis of studies related to his/her own country.

f) It would be of great benefit if a detailed teaching programme could be posted to the exchanges at the earliest opportunity with any infor ation that is available, giving an indication of depth or breadth of treatment, text-books normally used, project schemes, etc. The timetable itself may have to be provisional but it is unlikely that the subject areas will change much.

iii) Social and Domestic

a) The exchangee should be able to contact a committee within the College, who would be able to give advice and reasonable assistance when required.

b) The duties of the committee would be to:
   i) Make initial contact with the exchangee on his arrival in the country/city.
   ii) Provide a domestic introduction for the exc angee, eg, to the complexities of British stores, travel systems, domestic appliances and social arrangements.
   iii) Provide an introduction to the College: this would necessarily extend beyond the staff induction course, to include explanations of terms, course titles, examination systems, etc.
   iv) Provide a structure of 'other experiences', initially with other departments in the College and then with other institutions, in collaboration with the host department and with the exchangee.

c) The constitution of the committee to be:
   The Professional Tutor;
   A previous exchangee;
   A member of the American exchangee's department
      to act as guide counsellor;
   One other member of staff.

d) The exchange programme is more than a teacher exchange: it is also a social exchange. Thus the committee will be concerned with matters both academic and social/domestic, but on an informal basis.

Item 10.2

Guidelines for staff concerned with teacher exchange schemes

When an exchange teacher from another country joins our
college community it is important that we do all in our
power to make their stay with us a happy and worthwhile
year. A number of problems can arise from the exchange
scheme, eg from the likelihood that the exchangee will not
be able to replace his/her British counterpart completely
and, in the first few months, will be affected by a considerable culture shock. In order to alleviate such
problems, the following guidelines have been produced
for the various members of staff concerned with he exchange scheme. These guidelines should be read in conjunction with the policy statement for teacher exchange.

VICE PRINCIPAL

The Vice Principal will be concerned with:
Publishing details of the UK/US exchange scheme during
the summer term in each academic session and inviting
applications from potential exchangees;

Receiving applications from potential exchangees and
seeking assurances from departments, and from the
Principal, that any staffing problems that might arise
from an exchange can be resolved within the resources
of the college;

Circulating details of college applicants to associated
US colleges and seeking to obtain details of potential
exchangees from these colleges;

Circulating details of US applicants to college applicants
and to their departmental heads in order that the suitability of exchangees can be determined, by direct correspondence between the exchangees themselves and between
their respective heads of department where necessary;

Obtaining the written agreement of college exchangees
and their heads of department to proceed with the exchange
application;

Supervising the completion of the official exchange
application forms and their submission to the Central
Bureau for Educational Visits and Exchanges;

Informing the Central Bureau of the names and colleges
of the proposed US exchangees;

Obtaining approval, where necessary, of the Local Authority.

Where an exchange scheme is established with another
country, eg Austrailia, the Vice Principal would be concerned in a similar capacity.

147

KINGSTON COLLEGE OF FURTHER EDUCATION LIBRARY

Where an exchange is arranged on an individual basis the Vice Principal would be available to advise on the correct procedures to be adopted.

HEAD OF DEPARTMENT

Although the aims of the exchange scheme are wider than the needs of the host institution, it is important that a head of department consider first the effectiveness of the exchanges as a replacement member of staff, especially if the question of a single specialism exists. Thus it is essential that the head is involved from the beginning of the following aspects of the exchange scheme:

A. Prior to Acceptance of the Exchange:

Providing full details about the post in his department in conjunction with his member of staff applying for exchange;

Considering carefully the details of the foreign applicant;

Seeking further information if details received are not considered sufficient for the head to determine the suitability of the exchange, either through the potential exchangees themselves or through the head of department of the other college.

B. After Acceptance of the Exchange:

Providing adequate details about:

a) the syllabuses to be taught;
b) the normal teaching methods used, including any project schemes;
c) the text-books normally used;
d) assessment procedures, eg examination systems, continuous assessment, setting and marking of papers, etc;
e) any particular roles or duties involved, eg as course tutor;
f) teaching hours per week, taking due regard of the recommended reductions;
g) the college calendar for the year;
h) the general character of the student body;
j) the appointment of a tutor within the department to act as academic and administrative guide and counsellor.

(Much of the information under Section B can be supplemented and enlarged upon by the departmental member of staff.)

C. At college:

As part of the college induction course, which the exchange will attend the head or his deputy should discuss:

a) the administrative arrangements within the department;
b) the assistance that can be given within the college
   and department towards making the exchange a success
   in the broadest sense, eg arrangements for visits to
   other institutions, to functions arranged by the exchange bureaus, cultural visits, etc;
c) the opportunities that exist for exchangees to attend
   college committees, participate in staff association
   events and sporting activities, etc.

PROFESSIONAL TUTOR

Although basically the role of the professional tutor in
the exchange scheme is an informal one of providing information and giving advice and reasonable assistance
when requested, it is important that he ensures the
following functions are carried out, either personally or
by a member of the college committee concerned with the
exchange (ref section (iii) of the Policy Statement).

Arrangements are made for:
a) meeting the exchangee and family on arrival in the city;
b) keys to be available for entry to the house;
c) transport to be available to carry the family and
   luggage to their address;
d) friends or neighbours to be introduced as soon as
   possible;
e) the family to be shown the household, domestic and
   emergency services available;
f) visit to the local police in order to register;
g) introduction to the local schools as appropriate.

At college, the professional tutor will be concerned
with the exchangees on the Induction Course. In addition, however, he should ensure that:
a) appropriate introductions are made;
b) the head of department and departmental tutor provide
   any additional information that is required about the
   department and the college;
c) during the year, a structure of other experiences is
   provided, in conjunction with all those concerned in
   the exchange scheme.

it was felt that such experience could in fact be helpful in gaining promotion.

Teachers tended to stress the personal and domestic problems they encountered rather than academic or teaching ones. A major problem which was raised almost without exception was that of living on a British salary. One teacher who had an exchange position in Australia, stated that the union branch had had a 'whip round' for him. Most reported having taken on additional work, such as evening-class or summer-school teaching 'to make ends meet'. Those teachers who had children of school age thought that their education had not been seriously affected and commonly it was felt that they had enjoyed the year and benefited from the experience.

Although they had had to adjust to different working and living conditions most staff reported that they had experienced no great difficulty in settling down in a new institution and country. It was generally felt that overseas colleagues had been helpful, friendly and hospitable. Particular mention was made of the work of the Central Bureau in preparing staff for their future exchange and, without exception, teachers were of the opinion that extremely valuable help and advice had been obtained from this source. Teachers who expressed criticism of arrangements made tended to be those who had undertaken the organization of the placement themselves. Teachers in those colleges without formalized arrangements for exchanges considered it would be advantageous for a subcommittee to be set up to organize this and for college guidelines to be established. In particular staff who had organized their own exchange/placement felt that it was essential that a 'conditions of exchange' document should be drawn up for exchangees.

It was often said that seeing other approaches to teaching and educational management had led to a reassessment of British FE practice. Yet some exchangees reported that they felt frustrated on their return to find it was hard to implement any of the ideas, however small, that they had 'picked up' while overseas. Colleagues were considered on the whole to be uninterested in other educational systems and resistant to new practices. It is of interest that the two overseas teachers on exchange visits whom we interviewed also felt that this was the case. It was believed that rather more could be gained from exchanges if college staff were more prepared to discuss and examine some of the approaches taken by other countries to similar educational problems.

Senior staff in those colleges where exchanges had taken place stated that from their point of view the arrangements had worked well and that 'the disruption caused is not as much as you might expect'. The preliminary administrative work was seen as the most time-consuming part of the scheme. Those senior staff who had themselves taken short overseas visits sponsored by the Central Bureau and British Council thought that there could be positive results from contact with educators in other countries.

In the remaining fourteen colleges, exchanges and study visits had no recognized place within their staff development schemes. We found that the majority of teachers and some heads of department in these colleges were ignorant of the existing opportunities and one member of staff who had undertaken an exchange was even unaware of the help and advice which he could have obtained from the Central Bureau. Often heads were unconvinced of the value of such arrangements or doubted whether staff would be willing to participate. For example one head remarked 'we do not have the type of staff who would want to do that kind of thing'. Yet many of the staff at interview stated that they would welcome such an experience and expressed a keen interest in learning more about the schemes available. While some teachers regarded their present family commitments as precluding their personal participation in exchanges or overseas placements, only a small minority felt there was little to be gained from such programmes. Those visits and exchanges which had taken place in these colleges were very few in number and tended to be the result of individual initiative and planning. In three of the colleges it was reported that the possibility of promoting and establishing a regular exchange system was currently being examined.

Overview

Our findings indicate that overseas exchanges and visits are a much neglected form of staff development; they received scant attention in the majority of formal policy statements and were seldom listed in documents outlining opportunities for the development of college staff. In general it would appear that the senior staff and those with responsibility for staff development have yet to recognize the potential contribution of such activities. Interviews with teachers revealed that there was not so much a lack of interest in exchanges and visits as an ignorance of the schemes currently available. Both the Central Bureau and the League for the Exchange of Commonwealth Teachers stated that they would welcome more applications from the FE sector.

151

Managers as well as teachers are likely to gain from extending their knowledge of other educational systems and it is important that they too are thoroughly acquainted with the opportunities which exist. Although senior staff are likely to experience difficulties through being absent from their posts for as long as a term or one year, short study visits may prove useful to them in formulating and reviewing college policy and practice. Indeed, given that at present there are limited opportunities for management development, current schemes for foreign visits should not be overlooked. Since professional tutors and staff development officers are likely to be consulted regarding current schemes it would seem beneficial that they, too, should have firsthand knowledge of their operation.

For overseas exchanges and visits to become an established part of development programmes it is necessary for information on them to be well publicized within each FE institution. Where staff development interviews are held staff could be encouraged to consider such possibilities alongside those for further study and other types of training. Guidelines may also need to be established in those colleges regularly participating in exchanges so that procedures and responsibilities are clarified. The guidelines drawn up by one of the study colleges and reproduced earlier demonstrates how responsibilities for exchanges might be delineated. If colleges are to maximise the benefit derived from participation in visit and exchange schemes it would seem desirable that staff with such experience should be called upon to describe foreign educational policies and practices with a view to discussing their relevance to the college. Meetings for this purpose could be organized and would themselves be a form of staff development.

CHAPTER 11

Curriculum development

The idea that curriculum development and staff development are closely linked is not new. As Coles has commented in connection with the training of university lecturers: 'Staff development is a natural outcome of and paradoxically a necessary prerequisite for curriculum development' (1977, p316). In FE the introduction of TEC and BEC courses and changes in the student population resulting from the introduction of YOP and UVP schemes, as well as the increasing numbers of students with special needs, have meant that radical changes have been proposed in curricula and methods. A large number of staff are involved in preparing and teaching new courses and it has been suggested that these developments have challenged 'the basic philosophy', aims and methods of traditional further education' requiring 'a new and different role for many lecturers' (Owen, 1971, p45). One aspect of our research was to discover how lecturers were coping with curriculum innovations and with the changing student population. The preparation they had received, any problems caused, and the type of staff development activity that was seen as promoting successful curriculum development were all investigated. This chapter discusses some of the major innovations in turn.

The introduction of TEC courses

The Technician and Business Education Councils were set up in 1973 and 1974 respectively, as a result of the report of the Haslegrave Committee (1969), to introduce a new national system of courses for technician and business education. All the colleges we visited were running TEC courses: some were among the first in the country to do so and had almost completed the changeover; others were in the throes of replacing one or two courses with TEC equivalents. Teachers' views on the introduction of TEC, the benefits and problems it created were remarkably

153

similar in all the colleges, although in those with greater experience of TEC, staff felt they were beginning to 'iron out some of the teething troubles' and 'see light at the end of the tunnel'.

A complaint of almost all the staff we interviewed was of the enormous burden that preparation for TEC placed on all those involved. Some lecturers complained that the confusion caused by TEC guidelines had made the task of designing courses even more difficult. Junior staff often seemed genuinely surprised that we asked them about preparation for TEC and other new course developments in connection with staff development. Many had attended no courses related to this work and did not feel that their curriculum development work was an inherent form of staff development. Since the types of problems that these staff emphasized reflect their development needs and the way TEC courses have altered teachers' roles, these problems will be discussed briefly before considering the availability of related staff development provision.

It is perhaps natural that TEC should have experienced some initial difficulties in communicating its intentions to colleges, yet the general feeling of teachers was that the speed of introduction, and too hastily conceived instructions and standard units meant the changeover had begun badly and had antagonized staff. The fact that TEC modified its validation procedure in mid-1976 testifies to the strength of dissatisfaction within FE as a whole with the original lengthy process. Despite this move we still heard complaints about the complications of gaining approval for a course and the amount of administrative work involved. In the view of senior staff members the Council and colleges had underestimated the degree of change required and it had not been made sufficiently clear to teachers that 'they would not be doing things the same way as they have in the past'.

The choice of staff to prepare TEC submissions and develop curricula was frequently criticised. In some cases teachers suggested that 'a select few' had been involved while other staff, although concerned with running the course, were not consulted. Senior staff generally refuted such claims arguing that 'the involvement of all staff who are to teach on such courses in the practical planning stages was regarded as part and parcel of the arrangements for staff to prepare for new courses'.

The amount of remission to prepare for TEC courses was a particularly sore point in every college we visited. It was said by the majority of our respondents at both junior and senior levels to be either totally inadequate or non-existent. In one college only one lecturer in charge of a TEC course had been given an hour's remission from class contact, while other teachers had had to carry out the necessary work preparing TEC submissions, course materials, and later carrying out the testing procedures and associated administration in their own time. In a more typical college, course co-ordinators were the first to be given any remission available, but other teachers generally received no reduction in class contact for their work.

Teachers were, with few exceptions, concerned about the assessment arrangements for TEC units. Placing the responsibility for testing with colleges themselves (so increasing the administrative workload) and the use of phased testing throughout the year instead of a single final examination were the most common sources of dissatisfaction.

The requirement that TEC courses are written in terms of objectives was an additional subject of concern. Teachers who had never met the concept often found it difficult to grasp. Others said either that they had always written courses in this way, although perhaps never giving the method any name, or were familiar with the concept because of its introduction in Certificate in Education or CGLI 732 courses.

Concern was also expressed that employers were still unsure of TEC qualifications and that there was a need for colleges to communicate the implications of TEC more fully to firms. Given the pressure on staff to develop new courses and assessment procedures it is not surprising that increasing employers' knowledge of the new courses should have taken a low priority in many colleges. As more students leave with TEC qualifications, employers' ignorance may diminish, but obviously both the colleges and TEC itself will need to keep them informed. A widespread view was that many employers have shown little interest in the implications of the changeover to TEC and it was reported that few of them accepted inviations to be involved in planning college-designed units, which they tended to regard as 'college business'.

In two colleges early initiatives had been taken to encourage staff to take the City and Guilds 732 Achievement Testing Course. Here teachers felt less daunted by the task of setting behavioural objectives for each course. As one principal commented 'attendance at conferences held in the early days of these two developments (TEC and

BEC) meant that we were fairly fully informed of the sort of work that was going to be expected of us'. A number of teachers in these and in other colleges recommended the conferences run by Coombe Lodge as providing useful practical advice on how to write TEC courses and carry out student assessments. It was generally felt that these particular conferences dealt with exactly the sorts of problems teachers had encountered, and enabled staff to exchange experience and knowledge about TEC procedures. Usually it was said that only lecturers with responsibility for co-ordinating TEC programmes were sent to Coombe Lodge, although some colleges appear to have been able to send more than one member of staff. It was generally felt that more staff should have been given the opportunity to attend, though they recognized that Coombe Lodge could not be expected to cater for all those who wanted instruction.

Typically, senior staff said that when lecturers returned from a course or conference on TEC they were often asked to run a workshop for their colleagues. Most colleges also encouraged teachers to visit other local colleges which had already introduced TEC courses.

In three colleges more formal in-house courses had been arranged to familiarize teachers with TEC. In one the professional tutor had run three short courses for departments starting TEC - one each for general studies, construction and catering. In a second college the PL in charge of the Education Department ran a similar series after being approached by an individual member of staff. He felt, however, that the series should have been initiated by the Board of Studies at an earlier date. In a third a group of lecturers who had built up some expertise since 1976 in preparing submissions for both TEC and BEC were considering offering programmes in course design to colleagues in departments about to introduce new courses. This would no doubt meet with approval from teachers who complained of the wasteful repetition of effort when each department worked separately on its TEC submission.

The majority of RACs reported having mounted workshops, short courses or conferences to introduce teachers to TEC philosophy and procedures and, in some cases, to produce regional submissions. One RAC, however, felt that such support was outside its responsibility for FE teacher training, while another was currently considering whether its examining body should initiate such support. In several cases development activities had been organized for a few subjects only, while other subject submissions and related activites were left to individual college departments.

Besides Coombe Lodge courses and those organized by the
RACs, individual teachers mentioned that they had attended
courses on TEC run at local polytechnics and colleges of
education (technical). Several teachers said they had
found little difficulty in writing courses using objectives since the Certificate in Education course had prepared them for this. However, a number of suggestions
were made for possible improvements in existing courses
or for other types of provision. Most of our respondents
agreed that courses had often come too late to ease initial problems and that what was now needed was help and
advice with the second stage of TEC implementation and
running.

It was suggested that courses should be provided in 'the
different philosophies behind TEC and BEC' as well as
'course geared to specialist needs of teachers in subject
areas and in similar course levels across subject and departmental boundaries'. Such comments illustrate how
limited provision had been in the past, since many of the
teachers were unaware that such courses were already run
in other parts of the country. Perhaps the complaint
that courses introducing TEC were only available to senior
staff members explains why requests for these were made by
many junior teachers some years after the introduction of
TEC. Once TEC courses were over the early 'teething
troubles', the prime need felt by the majority of teachers
was for informal discussions with other teachers directly
involved in running similar schemes and with TEC officials
in order to share experiences and seek advice on specific
problems.

The introduction of BEC courses

It might be expected that the introduction of BEC courses
would cause staff fewer problems than TEC, since by the
time BEC was introduced colleges would have recognized
the amount of extra work necessary to develop TEC courses
and could anticipate some of the problems and resources
needed. The decision by BEC initially to undertake its
own course development rather than ask colleges to
develop their own units should also have reduced the
pressure on colleges changing to BEC. Colleges were
given the option to submit courses they had designed for
validation if there were special circumstances, but
generally they were encouraged to use standard units for
the first few years until they had built up expertise.

In practice, when asked about the introduction of BEC
courses, staff in business departments were as critical

as teachers involved in TEC provision, particularly concerning the amount of extra work the changeover had created. Problems generally centred around the increased workload involved in preparing and assessing schemes without remission from class contact and the difficulty of understanding 'BEC philosophy'. One head of Management and Business Studies commented that, because the college catered for all levels of BEC, his staff had little or no time for any other forms of staff development, and this situation would continue for at least five years until BEC has become established and the problems of introduction had been solved. This view was shared by junior staff; as one commented, 'everything revolves around BEC and this leads to the neglect of other students'.

Not all the colleges had been under such pressure - in one case a head of Business Studies stated that his staff had been able to spend a year preparing for the change and because 'objectives' were devised by BEC the department had few difficulties coping with the new approach. In another college the head of department involved felt that his department had been lucky; it had an unbalanced workload since a great deal of CSE and TSD work had finished at Easter leaving staff free to use the time available to prepare for BEC. Junior staff were, however, more likely to feel that BEC had increased their workload considerably since preparation had to be carried out in their own time. The demand by NATFHE for a reduction in class contact hours for those involved in TEC and BEC courses was considered by the majority of staff to be long overdue and some felt that NATFHE should have offered more encouragement to colleges to refuse to implement the changes without an agreement on remission. Most junior lecturers felt that although BEC courses had been consolidated during the first year and much had been learnt by mistakes made, a number of problems still remained and ironing these out would continue to take up a great deal of teachers' time and effort in the next few years.

Senior staff reported that they had a limited amount of remission to give to teachers and tried to distribute this as equitably as possible. Inevitably this meant that some teachers did not receive remission and their goodwill and willingness to carry the extra work in their own time was increasingly taken for granted. In one department the head said that staff had agreed to use all the remission available (20 hours) for BEC development in the first year. In another college NATFHE was negotiating an additional post with the LEA in an attempt to gain some recognition of the extra workload created by

BEC. The head of department in this case felt that this was only fair since 'BEC and the LEA have had hundreds of hours of staff time completely free of charge'. As with TEC, a minority disagreed with such sentiments, arguing that teachers should be expected to develop courses when they were not teaching.

Although assessment is much less the responsibility of college staff for BEC than for TEC, the procedures still came in for some criticism. It was suggested that there was widespread dissatisfaction at the methods of assessment which were 'too subjective'. The detailed monitoring required by BEC, including the preparation of student profiles and assignment matrices, was felt to be too time-consuming and staff were unlikely to be able to find time to carry it out properly.

Again, as in the case of TEC courses, teachers were convinced that the success of BEC would depend on employers' accepting the new qualifications. Disappointingly, it was reported that few of the employers invited to attend initial planning committees had accepted, and obtaining employer cooperation was becoming increasingly difficult since the financial climate made commercial concerns reluctant to release valuable staff.

The amount of preparation staff received to prepare for BEC varied between colleges and individuals within colleges. The majority of senior staff responsible for introducing BEC claimed that as many teachers as possible were sent to any relevant courses, conferences or workshops, and most teachers were said to have attended at least one course. Colleges reported that they had sent staff to local courses organized by the RACs, LEAs or to nationally run ones such as those at Coombe Lodge. In fact the majority of RACs reported that they had run a series of conferences or workshops to introduce BEC to colleges although, as for TEC, two RACs felt this was outside their remit. Some of these courses had been organized by the regional examining body and in a number of cases it was stated that BEC matters were a standing item on the agenda of appropriate subject subcommittees of the RAC. In two RACs follow-up conferences had also been held so that staff could discuss the progress of BEC courses and any administrative problems encountered. The extent of this regional preparation in fact varied from four one-day conferences to a complete series of regional and subregional working parties formed to develop joint courses over a period.

This varietyof regional provision was reflected in the

comments of staff who said they had been able to exchange experiences of introducing and running BEC with colleagues in other colleges. In one college it was reported that staff had been formally involved in organizing local courses on BEC for other colleges, but contacts were more often informal ones as a result of visits to other colleges or because of chance contacts at conferences. It was reported that despite the lack of remission to prepare BEC courses, expenses were paid and release granted in term time to allow teachers in one college to meet staff from other local institutions already involved in BEC. This exchange of views seems to be particularly welcome. Staff in a college, which had established no such links, felt very isolated in their efforts to develop a BEC scheme.

The majority of teachers who had attended Coombe Lodge conferences recommended them as being a helpful introduction to BEC. These conferences had been run on a five-day residential basis and were organized in a similar way to the TEC conferences. Courses on BEC organized by RACs, colleges of educational or other bodies were also recommended by most staff, but the total number of lecturers who had been able to attend was small in comparison with the number involved in BEC. Many teachers also felt that a one-day or short course could not possibly be sufficient development to cope with all BEC changes. The feeling that short courses can seldom answer all the problems associated with new curriculum development was not seen as restricted to TEC and BEC: 'there is a need for more second-stage courses generally, and although course members often express such a wish at the plenary sessions of conferences there rarely appears to be any follow-up'.

A small number of colleges reported having run in-house workshops to brief staff on BEC and established committees or working groups who met regularly to discuss the courses. A novel approach was adopted in one college where a residential weekend was organized by the Business Studies Department and supported by a £700 allocation from the LEA. A variety of teaching methods were employed, including formal presentations and syndicate group work. Alternative sessions were arranged at some points for those staff involved in BEC Higher National courses. Holding the course at a holiday resort may have helped make it more attractive, but staff involved in its organization clearly felt it had been successful. As the college principal wrote following the course: 'a residential provision for curriculum development is considered essential in view of the broad range of courses with which staff are involved and their isolation from colleagues in other colleges except on a regional basis.

The introduction of UVP

In July 1976 the Government issued a statement which proposed a programme of experimental schemes of vocational
preparation designed specifically for young people who
had left school and entered jobs where they received
little or no systematic education or training. This
programme was to combine educational and training elements
and its name - Unified Vocational Preparation - reflected
this intention.

The Sudale Report recommended that, for the success of
vocational preparation, staff involved should be trained
in 'appropriate teaching/learning methods and in counselling' and this training 'should be provided both before
and during the course' although it need not 'necessarily
be elaborate or extended' (DES, 1976, p10). In 1978 the
Further Education Curriculum Review and Development Unit
(FEU) published suggestions for staff setting up schemes,
while the consultative paper 'A Better Start in Working
Life' (DES et al, 1979) outlined proposals for extending
UVP provision, and put forward a number of suggestions
for the development of staff. These included introductory
courses or short workshops to familiarize teachers with no
experience of vocational preparation and a series of short
courses on specific aspects for more experienced staff. It
was stressed that 'staff development for vocational preparation, like vocational preparation itself, should
ideally take place as far as possible on the job' (p24).
Thus in-house courses were advocated as well as national
and regional initiatives. The paper suggested that a
number of organizations would need to be involved in
staff development for curriculum development associated
with the work including the ITBs, youth service, careers
service, colleges of education (technical) and polytechnic and university departments.

The development of tutors on UVP programmes has, then,
been the subject of some discussion. However, the varied
experience of UVP teachers in the colleges we studied
suggested that a national scheme for developing appropriate skills within FE colleges is still far from being
realized.

Twelve of the nineteen colleges were involved in UVP
schemes, but most had only recently established schemes.
Staff in these colleges were, as yet, unsure of how the
courses would develop and were only beginning to discover
how their teaching was affected. In four colleges, including two we studied in detail during the second stage

of the research, UVP schemes had been set up for some
time and had grown considerably. In these colleges,
teachers' greater experience meant that they were much
more concerned about the day-to-day running and curriculum implications of UVP than about questions of establishing a scheme. It was suggested that these courses
required a new approach which was unfamiliar to FE staff,
and that the structure of courses requiring staff to work
outside the college was difficult to incorporate into
traditional college timetables. Many UVP tutors said
that colleagues often regarded teaching outside the
college as 'a skive' as it increased the teaching load
of those left in the college. They were themselves convinced that the success of UVP schemes greatly depends
on college staff going to firms to teach. By meeting
the students on thier own territory it was easier both
to obtain their cooperation and to establish the relevance
of the scheme to their jobs.

It was generally reported that staff were chosen to teach
on these schemes because of their sympathy towards this
type of work and their flexibility. As a major role of
FE in UVP programmes is to provide training in social and
life skills as they relate to the working environment,
general studies departments were the most likely to be
involved, despite having already been heavily involved in
other new curriculum developments. In some cases the
choice of staff either to organize or teach on UVP courses
was said to occur by chance or by necessity, since no
other staff were qualified or available. Several problems
occurred when organizers tried to build up a team of
tutors. It was suggested that the number of teachers interested in this work was limited either because of its
low-level (and the effects of this on promotion prospects)
or because many teachers were reluctant to tackle a new
group of students and adopt a broader approach to teaching.
Teachers with adequate experience were often too senior
for the grade of post open, and many schemes were forced
to depend heavily on part-time staff, with all the associated difficulties in training, co-ordination and long-
term planning.

Each scheme is overseen by a committee made up of representatives from the firms, colleges and agencies involved.
This, together with visits to teach on employers'
premises had greatly increased contacts with local industry - a fact which was regarded as a positive outcome
of the scheme, even though tutors workloads were not ad-
justed to cope with this. Interestingly, it was suggested
that increased contact with industry had enabled UVP
tutors to 'cross to the training world', and a small

minority of the teachers we talked to were considering the possibility of leaving FE and taking up posts as trainers in industry.

The degree of preparation and training tutors received both before mounting UVP schemes and during their initial stages, varied between the colleges we studied. The FEU's (1978) suggestions for organizers of schemes drew on the experiences of tutors on pilot schemes; these tutors were themselves very much alone when developing the first UVP provision. For instance, in one college the tutor in charge of UVP said that he had received no formal training and had learnt solely by experience. He was now training other staff, not because senior staff had asked him to do this, but because he felt this was part of his job. The form this training took reflected his own approach to UVP - new tutors were initially allowed to observe a more experienced tutor in class and gradually given more responsibility. Aspects of teacher training courses were felt to be hlepful, but industrial experience was generally considered to be more important, and it was suggested that tutors without such experience should spend a short period in the firm running the UVP course to become familiar with the problems facing their students. Staff in this college had been afforded no opportunity to attend external courses relating to aspects of UVP.

In other colleges it was reported that local or regional courses had been run to assist in setting up UVP schemes. Such courses were organized by a variety of bodies: RACs, colleges of education (technical), industrial training boards or local college consortia. This provision was welcomed, although it generally appeared to consist of one-off courses of one or two days designed to encourage colleges to set up UVP schemes and it was suggested that more long-term development opportunities were needed. These might take the form of informal discussion groups involving a number of colleges since the small size of UVP teams means that staff tend to feel isolated and lacking opportunities to compare approaches with staff in other colleges. Personnel from the firms involved in UVP might also benefit from attending short courses to develop schemes. Informal discussion meetings rather than formal courses appeared to be more favoured by the teachers themselves. Staff in one of the colleges we studied had taken part in the staff development project sponsored by the Inter-Departmental Group (IDG) and organized by Yorkshire and Humberside Council for Further Education. This project resulted from a series of regional and national workshops organized in 1978 by the

IDG to help staff involved in UVP work, or about to become involved, with the approach and organization of a scheme. As well as involving teachers on UVP schemes, teachers working on TRADEC courses (which are similar in many ways to UVP courses) were also encouraged to attend. The workshops were much appreciated by the teachers involved. As one lecturer in a General Studies department who had attended the workshops commented; compared with the introduction of BEC in the college, much more thought and resources appeared to have been given to the planning and implementation of UVP This reaction is, however, an exception. In general terms support provision at RAC level was variable, while in-house support often amounted to little or nothing and was most certainly not commensurate with need. Few systematic attempts had been made at the college level to assess teachers' specific new needs in relation to the demands being made for team collaboration, student-centred learning, innovative teaching and assessment methods, counselling and guidance. Despite the large numbers of part-time staff employed in this area, the problems of creating mechanisms to ensure their involvement in curriculum and staff development had not been faced. It was, then, impossible for staff development provision to be tailored accordingly. In essence, expertise is having to be developed by experience.

The introduction of YOP

The Youth Opportunities Programme was established under the Special Programmes Division of the Manpower Services Commission in 1978 to provide an integrated range of training schemes and courses for unemployed young people aged 16-19. Its chief aims were to offer a constructive alternative to these young people and to improve their working prospects. YOP offers a wide range of work preparation courses and work experience schemes tailored to individual and local needs. All courses are designed locally within a nationally agreed curricular framework. The FE sector is able to contribute to YOP not only by providing work preparation courses and educational support for those in work experience placements, but also be assisting with staff training, co-ordinating integrated schemes of work preparation and work experience, and offering an educational consultancy service to other bodies and individuals involved in YOP provision.

At the time of our study, thirteen of our sample colleges had introduced YOP schemes. Very few teachers reported having received preparation for this work. The rapid introduction of college schemes had meant that suitable curricula and teaching approaches were often chosen by trail and error, and teachers regretted that there had been little time to consider in more detail the most appropriate strategies and curricula before courses started. The burden of curriculum development on YOP most affected teachers in General Studies departments who provided social and life skills courses. These same staff had often already been involved in developing similar components for TEC, BEC and UVP programmes, but different approaches needed to be adopted to cater for this group. As one head of general education commented 'many of the staff in my department are lurching from one new development to the next with very little time to evaluate what they are doing'.

Difficulties encountered in introducing YOP programmes tended initially to be concerned with accommodation and staffing. Most colleges found considerable difficulty in finding separate classrooms for YOP students. In one college a new department was established as a result of the introduction of this work. In a second college the expansion of both YOP and UVP work meant that the general education department had so grown in size that it was in the process of being divided - one half to cope with this work, the other to offer traditional FE courses. In a third college all courses for the MSC, including YOP, are run on an extra-departmental basis through an organizer who is directly responsible to the principal. The staff interviewed claimed that they had had to hold meetings at the homes of individual teachers since this was the only way they could all meet to discuss the courses, because of timetable clashes, the problems caused by split sites and the difficulty emphasized by all our respondents of lack of time.

In the general climate of 'cutbacks' the expansion of this work was seen by some as a threat to other courses. In contrast, teachers actually involved in YOP were convinced that they received fewer college resources in terms of remission, staff development opportunities and promotion: the low level ascribed to YOP and similar courses by Burnham, with the associated reduced chances for promotion, was regarded by most teachers as unjustifiable. Some anticipated that they would have to abandon YOP work to enhance their career prospects. The practice of employing teachers on YOP courses on one-year contracts was also criticized as discouraging staff from taking on this work and making any long-term course planning impossible.

Mention was frequently made of the paradox inherent in developing MSC work: on the one hand, the MSC had undoubtedly brought a fresh impetus to colleges engaged in providing courses for students in the lower ability ranges;

165

on the other hand, it was suggested that initiatives in
this area had been stultified by efforts made to remain
within MSC guidelines when new courses were being devised.
Thus, teachers were worried that the literacy and numeracy
components of their courses were too small to meet
students' needs adequately - a situation created by the
need not to raise the 'educational' element of a course
too high to attract MSC funding. Similarly, it was argued
that local education authorities were beginning to look
unfavourably on courses which were unlikely to meet MSC
demands.

Few of the colleges we studied provided any systematic
training for staff involved in YOP courses. Teachers
themselves were particularly concerned about their lack
of training in counselling and assessment and about the
dearth of suitable courses designed to tackle the problems encountered with unmotivated students.

Some colleges had provided staff to act as consultants to
other local insitutions as their expertise in running the
new types of course has grown; in one college the lecturers involved in YOP implementation were asked to hold a
course for other staff in their locality. The Numeracy
Project based at Westminster College had provided assistance to ILEA colleges and staff involved in courses
similar to YOP were encouraged to attend weekend courses
on numeracy and literacy. Outside London such provision
is more sporadic, and YOP staff often said they felt isolated both from others teaching on similar courses and
from schools and industrial agencies associated with the
programme. In one college we visited, the exceptional
interest of the principal and the head of department
concerned meant that staff had been encouraged to attend
a number of relevant courses. Yet it was interesting to
discover that teachers said they were becoming increasingly reluctant to continue to follow this type of development. This reflected to some extent the increasing
confidence of this group of teachers in their own approach,
but also stemmed from a perceived need for more informal
discussion with other staff regarding their approach
rather than for a taught course.

As with UVP - whose teachers' needs are in many ways
similar to those engaged on YOP courses - it was frequently
reported that college management seemed often not to ack-
nowledge the need for additional support for teachers involved in vocational preparation work. This was seen as
reflected in the low esteem accorded to the area and in
the fact that little or no time allowances were given
either for curriculum development or staff training. It

may be argued that colleges can legitimately regard non-contact hours as available for this purpose. It should, however, be remembered that most vocational preparation courses are taught by lecturers grade I and part-time staff who have the smallest allowances of non-contact time. Thus, any success achieved in this area depends largely on the enthusiasm and commitment of small, often isolated, groups of teachers without much power in the college hierarchy and frequently without the encouragement of colleagues.

Students with special educational needs

Until the mid-1970s there was little provision in mainstream colleges for young people with special needs. With few exceptions, students who were admitted had to be able bodied and to have reached a minimum educational standard. In more recent years - particularly since the publication of the Warnock Report (1978) - it has been increasingly recognized that the further education sector has an important role to play in assisting these young people through the transition from school to adult life. Some colleges have responded by developing special courses and units or by ensuring that normal courses are accessible to these students; others have few specialist facilities and can offer only limited provision. The colleges in our study reflected this wide range. Most had one or two physically handicapped students attending mainstream courses, and in some cases students with moderate learning difficulties had transferred to YOP classes from special schools. One college was developing a home-link scheme whereby volunteer tutors visited students in their own homes on an outreach basis. Three of the colleges had created more extensive provision, including a residential unit for physically handicapped students, a two-year work preparation course and a three-year 'daily living'course for special school leavers.

Five colleges had designated a member of staff as responsible for ensuring that the needs of handicapped students were being met, but these individuals did not as a rule fulfil the role envisaged for them by Warnock whereby they would also perform a dynamic staff development function in increasing their colleagues' understanding and knowledge of special needs. Two colleges ran the CGLI 731 course for teachers of the handicapped, but in most of the other colleges priority was given to the physical needs of students, while special training for the staff teaching them was less frequently considered. Where the number of students with special needs was still small, interested and sympathetic staff were often believed to be sufficient without the added necessity for specific training programmes. However, senior members of staff in several colleges did say that they were aware that lecturers involved in this work might need special support and training. Conferences and workshops organized by RACs and LEAs to discuss the implications of the Warnock Report appeared to have increased general awareness of the needs of both students and their teachers, but in some colleges it was argued that further provision or staff training was hampered by a lack of resources.

Financial constraints have already imposed restrictions on the number of teachers attending all types of course, but staff with major commitments to students with special needs felt that their development in particular was generally accorded low priority. There are in any case relatively few systematic training schemes that are of particular relevance to these teachers. While further education for the handicapped features regularly on conference and short course programmes, there is sparse input on this topic in initial training courses or post-experience programmes.

In practice, teachers with major responsibility for work in this area have a variety of training needs deriving from their different levels of experience and expertise. The course most commonly followed by lecturers in our study was the CGLI 731, though it was recognized that a single course could not hope to cater fully for the highly diverse needs of all those following it. In addition, many had attended conferences, short courses and workshops organized on a local or regional basis. The majority had found these useful, particularly since they had allowed them to establish contacts with others working in the area. However, it was reported that at a conference organized for staff from both schools and colleges little time had been made available for a discussion of FE's role; it had merely been agreed that FE should make **provision for** the handicapped. Several lecturers said they felt very isolated and would welcome more contact with other colleges which had made provision for the handicapped. They tried to attend any conference or course which seemed relevant to teaching handicapped students, even if this meant giving up free time or vacations. As a group, these teachers appeared to be particularly dedicated to their work and willing to take up any development opportunities available despite what they perceived as limited support from their colleges. Several individuals had set out to improve their knowledge and expertise on their own initiative, for instance by following the Open University course on 'The Handicapped Person

168

in the Community'. Others had pursued the idea of self-help by team teaching or by holding informal group meetings to share ideas and discuss common problems.

Within individual colleges the notion of increased liaison and co-operation was seen as taking on added importance in relation to provision for students with special needs. The strict departmental structure within which colleges have been traditionally organized must be broken down to offer balanced multidisciplinary provision which crosses departmental lines. In many instances this is a new departure for FE teachers who must consequently develop new patterns of working to ensure the continuity of students' learning experiences. Staff frequently pointed out that at the present time it was often difficult to co-ordinate course elements when they were taught in different departments which tended to be autonomous.

Staff responsible for organizing provision for handicapped students reported spending a great deal of time liaising with outside agencies to recruit students, find employers willing to take on students, and keep up to date with developments in other organizations involved in educating disabled young people. Finding new employers prepared to take students on work experience was more difficult each year. In general, curriculum development for students with special needs was regarded as presenting colleges with new problems whose solution might require a different starting point from the traditional course structure which focussed heavily on a specific vocational goal. It was, moreover, recognized that staff with the necessary experience and expertise to tackle this problem are in short supply. A staff development input on curriculum development was therefore seen by teachers with major responsibility for the design of courses as a matter of some urgency. This was also true of the whole area of assessment. Staff were generally aware of the particular importance of conducting careful monitoring of students with special needs, but they frequently acknowledged a need for significant improvement in this area of their work. FE as a whole has little experience in selecting and applying assessment procedures for these students, and the range in current practice is enormous. If the necessary improvements are to be made, assessment must become a more important element in teacher training programmes; and better consultative links must be established with external agencies to ensure an input of specialist help and advice.

The reluctance, and sometimes fear, felt by staff who have limited contact with students with special needs was seen by many teachers as the greatest obstacle to the successful integration of disabled young people into FE. It was anticipated that as staff came into contact with these students their fears and prejudices would gradually decrease. However, a number of teachers felt that more formal methods were needed, including in-house courses to inform lecturers of the needs of handicapped students and about the teaching methods which could help integrate them into mainstream classes. It was suggested that if sufficient numbers of staff were to be persuaded to attend such courses, they would have to be organized in college time. Induction courses were an obvious vehicle for this type of training, but experienced staff would also need to be made aware of these students' needs. Initial teacher-training courses run externally were also suggested in this context but again lecturers who did not wish to train or who had trained in the past, would be excluded from this provision. It was felt that the majority of FE lecturers should have some training in this area since current policies indicated that most would come into contact with many more handicapped students in future. Thus short in-house or local courses would need to be mounted to complement initial teacher training courses.

Often staff were said to be aware of the difficulties of access for physically handicapped students but oblivious to the problems of other types of disability. In practical subjects, lecturers often dismissed the possibility of having handicapped students in class because of safety regulations. Yet such problems could be overcome. More serious than physical access were the problems students experienced in keeping up with lecturers and taking down information. Yet these problems were rarely discussed. Any course aimed at increasing lecturers' awareness would need to tackle these problems and explain how specialist aids and alternative forms of lesson presentation could help students. First, staff would have to accept handicapped students and to do so would need to learn about their handicaps and how they differ. An important aspect of a successful approach to teaching handicapped students was an emphasis on their strengths rather than weaknesses. It was also suggested that few FE lecturers realize that the speed of the course, and not necessarily the speed of a lecturers' delivery, could adversely affect students' progress.

The CGLI 731 has had little success in attracting lecturers with limited contact and, indeed, it was apparent in all of the colleges we visited that many of these teachers were reluctant to attach priority to students with special

needs in the context of their own development plans. We
have already seen theat this reluctance may derive in part
in part from the small numbers of handicapped students as
yet taking non-specialized courses and from teachers'
apprehensions about the problems they might face with an
integrated class. There is also the fact that work with
these students generally falls into the category of non-
advanced. The effects of this in terms of salary, status
and career prospects has been mentioned earlier in relation to YOP and UVP schemes.

Overview

The introduction of new courses in the last few years
has involved staff in many departments in a great deal
of curriculum development work. The greater involvement
of teachers in planning their own curricula and assessment procedures, as well as the need to develop different
relationships with students and closer contact with industry, has radically changed the nature of many lecturers' work. It must, however, be said that FE is still a
long way from recognizing the need to establish a close
positive relationship between curriculum issues and staff
development. Teachers will only alter their approach if
they are convinced of the ncessity of doing so and are
helped to develop the requisite skills.

If curriculum innovations are to be successfully implemented, and so fully beneficial to students, a programme
of long-term and varied development opportunities is
needed for the staff involved. Our findings suggest
that existing development opportunities are variable in
quality but have generally met with teachers' approval.
In many cases staff reported that they were 'clutching
at straws' and would participate in 'anything that might
help'. The dearth of courses catering for different
levels of experience and competence is common to all
recent curriculum developments. Courses are still needed
to familiarize teaching staff new to these developments
with their background, methods and objectives; continuing
development opportunities are also needed to extend the
knowledge of staff who have been involved for some time.
A common complaint of teachers concerned the lack of
follow-up to existing courses. As one commentator has
suggested, 'a staggered course structure... little and
often, rather than once for all' (Astle, 1980, p9) might
be more successful in promoting lasting curriculum development.

Many junior staff appear to be unaware of the opportunities already available, and thus those organizing courses
may need to establish more effective ways of reaching

teachers directly involved in curriculum development work. With limited budgets it is obviously difficult to publicize courses, but more use could be made of college newssheets and similar publications.

As departments build expertise in curriculum development techniques, college-based courses, in which experienced staff help those new to course development with their work, have become more feasible. In practice, experience gained of curriculum development in one area is not disseminated throughout a college. Instead, teachers tend to operate in discrete groups so that the processes of learning by experience are repeated over and over again.

Our findings would, however, suggest that although there is an urgent need for more external courses combined with the increased use of college-based expertise, there is also a growing demand for liaison with staff from other colleges and agencies involved in similar work. Local and regional courses and Coombe Lodge conferences were seen as providing some opportunities for such contacts, and the experience of working in local consortia to develop TEC and BEC submissions was also felt to be valuable in encouraging more frequent contact between colleges than had been the case in the past. More formal and informal opportunities of this type whereby individuals could meet to discuss common problems and discover how others are working towards a solution would be welcomed. Such an approach might be expected to have particularly fruitful outcomes if it could be combined with what teachers often referred to as 'a comprehensive back-up service'. The FE Staff College, MSC, FEU and other national agencies as well as the local education authority advisers have a potentially useful role to play here.

It can be argued that any success achieved in recent curriculum innovations in FE has depended not so much on good staff development as on the commitment of a relatively small number of teachers who have been prepared to sacrifice their time to introduce new curricula and new approaches to teaching – and time is indeed a major constraint. In the case of lecturers involved in vocational preparation and in provision for students with special needs, they have been asked to sacrifice not only time but also their prospects for career advancement. There is still an urgent need for support in these areas and raising the status of this work would now appear essential if it is to compete for resources with more conventional forms of further education.

CHAPTER 12

Administration and management

With over 70,000 full-time teaching staff employed in the further education sector and almost twice this number employed on a part-time basis, the importance of effect- ive management is undeniable. Apart from co-ordinating the work of large numbers of staff and students, further education management now faces the task of responding to the many changes that are taking place in the sector. Official recognition of the need for further education management training came as early as 1957 with the pub- lication of the Willis Jackson Report, which recommended the creation of a residential Staff College and the est- ablishment of a permanent Advisory Committee for the Supply and Training of Teachers. More than twenty years later the FE Subcommittee of ACSTT was still pointing in its 1978 discussion document to an urgent need for improve- ment in both the quality and quantity of training provi- sion for managers at all levels. This document has never- theless been greeted with disappointment by FE staff who generally see it as insubstantial in its conclusions and lacking in practical guidelines for the implementation of its various recommendations. A statement from the National Association for Staff Development described it as 'at best a meagre preliminary to what should be an urgent discussion of a markedly neglected topic' (NASD, 1979,p1).

ACSTT recognised that their aim of developing a coherent system of training for further education staff would necessitate for many teachers 'a career long programme, within which appropriate elements of management training would be expected to have their place within initial training, post-experience training and advanced study levels' (ACSTT, 1978, p7). Nevertheless, in view of their opinion that 'the investment in management education and training for an individual member of staff should be commensurate with his management responsibilities' (Ibid, p8), priority was given in their recommendations to post-initial in-service training. The perhaps inevitable emphasis on the needs of staff of head of department status and above, together with the fact that in most colleges staff development is still highly identified with initial and post-experience training in the skills of *teaching*, means that the 'career-long programme' of management education seems to lie at some currently unspecified point in the future. The current concern about the provision of appropriate training in management and administration is not however simply a question of preparing teachers for promotion. As more staff become involved in the decision-making process, as more collaborative teaching and curriculum planning occur, teachers are finding that they need to extend their knowledge of planning procedures and organizational skills and to develop a greater awareness of management techniques. Those concerned with planning for the future of FE must therefore think in terms not of the education and training of managers occupying specific roles, but of preparing a variety of college personnel for the effective performance of administrative and managerial functions.

Formal training provision

Formal training in education management is provided by a variety of agencies, from the universities, polytechnics and colleges offering degree and diploma courses, to the DES, RACs and LEAs running a wide range of long and short courses on specialist topics. Major qualification-bearing programmes of training are relatively recent innovations which are still few in number. Full-time, part-time, day-release or block-release programmes of between one and three years' duration can lead to a master's degree or to a diploma in education management or in management studies. The curricula of these courses do, however, vary considerably from the more academic in content to those placing emphasis on the practical aspects of day-to-day managerial tasks.

Staff of head of department status and above were asked to recommend courses on the basis of their own experience of attendance. Courses run by industry were felt to be potentially useful to FE staff but probably too costly to be a practicable possibility for most teachers. Particular mention was made of Coombe Lodge conferences and the Diploma in Management studies, which is now offered by more than fifty FE colleges together with a number of extra-mural centres. Cantor and Roberts (1979) note that the DMS has been subject to considerable criticism on the grounds that it was not of sufficiently high quality.

This was not, however, reflected in the comments made by
staff in our study who had taken DMS courses, all of
whom mentioned the interpersonal relations aspects of
their course as being of particular value, while several
supported the view expressed by one teacher that 'taking
a course with non-educationists was extremely refreshing
and enlightening'. The fact that the roles of senior
staff can vary enormously from one institution to another
was frequently pointed out by vice-principals, who
generally felt that it was extremely difficult to design
a course that offered wide applicability to their operational needs. From a practical point of view, perhaps the
lesson to be learned here is that courses should not be
confined to attendance by staff of a stipulated grade,
but should instead be orientated towards particular management topics. The suggestions made by senior staff participating in our investigation would indicate that such
topics should include: interpersonal relations, counselling techniques, effective communications procedures,
delegation practices, and the management of financial
resources.

Staff below head of department level were asked to indicate the kinds of course they would like to see offered, but which are currently unavailable to them. Responses
to this question frequently included reference to courses
in aspects of administration and management. Overall,
staff at this level were far less likely to have had the
opportunity to attend courses of this type than their
colleagues at more senior grades. During the last five
years 20 per cent of principal lecturers, 13 per cent of
senior lecturers, 10 per cent of lecturers grade II, and
four per cent of lecturers grade I had attended a course
external to their institution. In the case of in-house
courses these percentages are reduced to 9,2,3 and 2
respectively, which represents only three per cent of
the entire sample of respondents at these grades. In
terms of both external and in-house courses the level of
attendance did not differ according to the sex of the
teacher or to the category of work taught. It is perhaps
worth noting at this point that staff at all grades were
often ignorant of many of the training opportunities
open to them. All had heard of the Coombe Lodge conferences, but were unsure of the existence of courses
run from other institutions. They largely tended to hear
of a particular course from a colleague who had taken it.
Unlike the information on initial teacher-training,
management training possibilities seem less likely to
filter through the normal channels of communication
within FE.

Regional initiatives

Seven RACs had established committees, subcommittees or
working parties for the specific purpose of considering
FE management training. Typical terms of reference
were: 'To collect information on current regional provision, identify needs and draw up a regional strategy
for provision'; while typical committee composition included representatives of local authorities, colleges,
HMI and, where applicable, staff from the regional management centres and former colleges of education (technical).
It should be noted that in two cases the working party
had already disbanded: one was simply *ad hoc* and had met
on only one occasion, while the other had disbanded 'on
recognizing the lack of resources for this training and
the low priority likely to be accorded it by local
authorities in the future'. In the three RACs where no
specific committee had been established, it was reported
that education management was part of the brief adopted
by the larger committee looking into the whole question
of FE teacher training.

As regards the formulation of policies in this area, four
RACs reported that the subject was still under discussion
and that no formal decision had yet been reached. In
another it had been resolved that 'any in-service training
for education management is likely to be on a college in-
house basis because of the lack of resources available'.
In the remaining RACs, although definite plans had still
to be finalized, it was clear that the Regional Management
Centres were to play a key role as providers. To assist
in their deliberations several RACs had also planned
short courses and conferences to serve the basically
diagnostic function of indicating which areas should be
given priority coverage in longer course provision.

While rationalization and co-ordination is obviously a
major concern at the regional level, it seems clear that
individual initiatives will still have their place within
any broader regional or national plan. By way of example,
the principal of one college is our study reported the
existence of a scheme which he regarded as far superior
to the courses currently available to him. All the
principals of the local colleges and polytechnics had
formed themselves into an association to facilitate discussion of problems relating to management and, where
possible, the adoption of a common policy. The worth of
this kind of approach was mentioned by several heads of
department, who greatly valued any opportunity to meet
with colleagues in other local institutions to discuss
their common problems. In particular, a one-day workshop

organized by the JCIC 'to explore the management dilemmas faced by participants' was cited as a very fruitful experience. Such informal joint-college initiatives would seem to present a most effective possibility - in terms of both cost and outcome - as a basis for expanding provision in the future. Three of the colleges in our sample reported that at the time of writing they were holding discussions with other colleges in the local authority with a view to exploring the possibility of running courses on a co-operative basis.

The Further Education Staff College

No discussion of further education management training would be complete without reference to the contribution made in this area by the FE Staff College. The Coombe Lodge Declaration of Trust describes its work as: 'for the purpose of improving the efficiency of establishments of further education there shall be provided for the senior members of the staffs of such establishments and for persons engaged in or connected with industry, commerce, universities, the civil service, local government and associated occupations, facilities for education, training and research, including facilities for the exchange of ideas, information and experience relating to further education' (para 1).

Over an academic year of some forty weeks the College offers a range of conferences each with a maximum intake of thirty-six members and an average take-up of 97 per cent (Birth, 1979). Their content falls into three broad categories: general college management, a systems approach to the management of the curriculum; and explorations of the practical implications of new developments affecting further education colleges. The central component of the management conference schedule can perhaps be regarded as the series of four one-week phased courses orientated towards the needs of heads of departments and their deputies. The four broad areas covered by these courses are: Improving the Efficiency of Departments; The Skills of Department Management; The Use of Resources; and Change and Development. Under present arrangements participants can complete the series over a number of years, as and when it is possible for them to obtain the necessary release from college. Although in theory the phases can be taken concurrently, staff generally feel unable to leave their departments for so long a period and many LEAs limit the number of conferences on FE staff member can attend in a given year. It should, however, be noted that the programme is currently being restructured to comprise a foundation conference

followed by several optional modules. Under the present
scheme a frequent criticism voiced by our interviewees
was that staff who are not able to attend phases concurrently have found that the lack of follow-up means
that they have been unable to consolidate their newly
acquired knowledge or to come back with questions after
reflecting on its implications. It is hoped that the
new modular structure will facilitate a more flexible
pattern of attendance and follow-up.

From the outset it was made clear that provision was to
be directed towards the needs of senior members of staff
(Willis Jackson, 1957, para 156; Coombe Lodge Declaration
of Trust, para 1). This is still predominantly, though
not exclusively, the case. Slightly over half of our
respondents at head of department status and above felt
that conference membership should be extended to provide
a greater cross-section of grades more representative of
the real college situation. In the heads' phased course
it is common for college principals to act as invited
speakers. A number of heads who had attended parts of
this course argued that they saw great advantage in also
hearing the views of lecturers grade I on their perceptions of the role and responsibilities of a head and how
effectively these had been performed in their own experience. Statistics supplied to the project by the
Staff College show that attendance on the phased course
is not in fact exclusively confined to heads of department and their deputies. Indeed, Coombe Lodge has
recognized the potential need for extending management
training by proposing the establishement of a number of
outposts in different parts of the country, but there
are no formal plans for this to be implemented at the
present time. 1981 did, however, see a new departure
whereby three study conferences held under the auspices
of the Staff College took place away from Coombe Lodge
itself. This may well set a pattern for the future.

Other providing agencies could also play a part in extending
provision. Their ability to do this will depend to a
large extent on the current controversy within FE over
the question of whether training should be undertaken
before or after appointment to a post with managerial
responsibility. There is some feeling that post-appoint-
ment courses seem most appropriate when employer sponsorship is involved, as it is quite common for teachers to
move to another college in order to gain promotion. This
argument is offered by those who hold with the view that
staff who have taken up development opportunities owe an
allegiance to the college supporting them. Training in
preparation for a new appointment was also seen by some

as raising the difficulty of heightening expectations
for promotion which may not be fulfilled. The majority
view, however, supported the ACSTT ideal of a career-
long programme of education management training. A
typical comment made by one principal in the context of
encouraging Coombe Lodge to take on more junior conference members was that, 'We in further education are
generally pretty poor at preparing people for management
roles. Staff must be trained in preparation for management and administration before they take office'.
Similarly, heads of department we interviewed often expressed the view that their attendance at Coombe Lodge
would have been of greater benefit had it begun before
taking up their present appointments.

There is clear agreement between Coombe Lodge governors
and FE staff in supporting the ACSTT recommendation that
increased provision must be seen as a matter of urgency.
Staff we interviewed frequently expressed concern about
the difficulty of actually obtaining a place on any given
management conference, particularly since they believed
that attendance at the Staff College might weigh in their
favour when applying for a more senior post. There is,
of course, one major conclusion to be drawn: there is
simply not enough management training to go around.
Senior staff in our sample frequently made the point that
however many conferences the Staff College is able to
organize, and however many participants it is able to
attract, the extent of this provision is still 'a drop in
the ocean' compared with the current and likely future
demand. Bearing this factor in mind, it has perhaps been
inevitable that Coombe Lodge conferences are generally of
short duration. Staff in our sample were clearly concerned about this, suggesting that in future provision should
be made for systematic follow-up training as part of a
continuous learning process. Clearly this would necessitate careful co-ordination among providing agencies, both
to avoid duplication and to ensure that all relevant topics
and types of training were being covered. In the meantime the myth is perpetuated that management education is
a 'one-off' exercise. A number of our respondents
commented on the prevalence of this myth: 'The idea that
four weeks should represent the entirety of an individual's
training in management is obviously absurd'; 'One four-
week course seems to be all that is needed to ensure the
credibility of a head of department'. Coombe Lodge staff
themselves are keen to dispel this myth and to encourage
FE managers to build upon the work undertaken during
study conferences as part of a long-term development
process.

Senior staff were asked in questionnaires and interview
sessions to outline the benefits they saw as accruing
from attendance at Coombe Lodge. The vast majority referred to the value of 'contacts established outside the
planned sessions. The comments of heads included: 'Discussions with colleagues from other institutions gave me the
comfort of realizing that I am not the only one in the
country with problems or with the difficulty of trying to
find the correct answers'; 'They provide an opportunity
to consider how parallel problems arise throughout FE and
how they are dealt with in different colleges by varying
methods'. Similar comments were also made by staff at
principal and vice-principal level: 'The contacts are
very valuable and the informal discussions often reveal-
ing'; 'It allows senior staff the opportunity to withdraw from their colleges and to discuss problems with
others who are in a similar situation'; 'We have incor-
porated into our own structure a number of developments
gleaned from discussions with staff from other institutions

It was widely advocated that provision could be made more
accessible if the concept of the Staff College was taken
to mean not a single institution but a network of 'outposts' at various different localities throughout the UK.
It was felt that such an arrangement would be particularly
beneficial in expanding provision for those at the course
co-ordinator or section leader level. Advocates of this
scheme further argued that the apparent chief benefit of
attendance at Coombe Lodge - the opportunity to discuss
common problems with colleagues from other colleges -
would be made accessible to much larger numbers of staff
at all grades. As already mentioned, Coombe Lodge, too,
would favour such an arrangement.

It was widely felt that an increase in provision along
these lines would enable more than one representative
from each college to attend a given course, and that this
would have particularly beneficial consequences. Staff
believed that there would be a greater likelihood that
participants would be able to implement any new ideas
gleaned from a course in the context of their own college
and would, moreover, be able to discuss with other
participants aspects of the course whose implications
became apparent only on their return to college. In considering these comments on implementation, it is important to bear in mind the remark made by one principal who
felt that he had gained useful new knowledge from attending courses and conferences on management, but that it
was 'difficult to assess their actual impact on practice
compared with ten years' experience as principal'.

Considerations of this kind are also important in interpreting the widespread belief that the actual content of Coombe Lodge conferences is of less relevance than the benefits arising from informal contacts. Coombe Lodge, in line with the recommendations of industrial management trainers, tends towards the view that tutors should play an essentially non-directive role. As the present director has noted, 'The effect for a participant in the work of the college must be to give an understanding of how he could operate with developmental frameworks previously unknown to him rather than suggest that he ought to do so' (Wheeler, 1978, p3). The tutors do, in fact, vary in the extent to which they espouse this practice, but the fact remains that this may be one element in an explanation of why participants see a greater input being made by their colleagues than by the staff tutors. It is argued that it is up to the conference members to make use of the opportunities they are given and to consider the advantages and disadvantages of the various management styles with which they are confronted. The non-directive approach can be, however, a perilous line to tread since it relies so heavily for its success on the sensitivity and receptiveness of individuals. Where conference participants are reticent to experiment with techniques which are new to them or unable to recognize weaknesses in their existing approach, an excellent opportunity can so easily be lost.

Another factor which, perhaps inevitably, has a distinct bearing on reactions to the conferences, is the participants' own subject specialism. Teachers of management studies, business studies and the social sciences were especially likely to cast a critical eye on the actual course content. Some staff were disappointed that the emphasis appears to be very much on practice with the minimum of theoretical background. Moreover it was argued that such an approach was not conducive to real understanding of the issues and implications involved. In contrast, staff with other backgrounds appreciated that the course was 'not too theoretical'. Perhaps, as with initial teacher training courses, there is a greater need for all providers of FE management training to see flexibility as a central component in their thinking if they are to respond effectively to the demands of a highly diverse population.

In fact the staff tutors consider the constant reappraisal of their approach to be an important element of their work. Since it is impossible for them to obtain any precise objective measure of their impact on further education management, the most obvious evaluation technique at their disposal is to ask conference members for their views. Certainly this is done, but one problem relating to the task of evaluation was suggested by a number of staff who had themselves been conference participants. During the course of a week-long conference the staff tutors go to some lengths to establish an informal, friendly atmosphere which - while in itself laudable - means that 'it is extremely difficult to criticise without appearing ungrateful'.

It was frequently suggested during our field visits to colleges that the fact that the conference programmes are prepared and presented by resident staff diminished their immediacy and impact and created a credibility gap between the tutors and conference members. The reason for this situation was expressed as 'the remoteness of the staff tutors from grass roots FE practice'. It was, moreover, felt that the design of conferences was becoming too mechanistic and lacking in innovativeness. To counter these perceived problems it was suggested that more extensive use should be made of secondment to recruit tutors with recent experience of working within further education colleges. Clearly it is critical to the staff college concept that its tutors be viewed as being in touch with the realities of college life. At present the Staff College claims that this is achieved by ongoing contact with conference members, research, consultation, and external committee membership, together with the practice of inviting outside speakers and supplementing the resident staff with temporary associate tutors.

The deputy director has said of the College that, 'Its contribution to research and development, case study collection, off-campus committees, articles and other publications would stand comparison with most university departments and would rank above the majority of polytechnic departments' (Birch, 1979, p11). It was argued by senior staff in our sample that rather than increasing these activities, Coombe Lodge tutors could make a more valuable contribution to further education management training if they were to expand their current advisory service and concentrate on working jointly with college staff on programmes of training to be run at institutional or regional levels. Certain colleges are currently attempting to offer such programmes for their own staff in the knowledge that it will not be possible for Coombe Lodge to meet the demand for places in the context of the present arangement. The Staff College advisory service clearly has a potentially wider contribution to make in the future in assisting colleges to design and set up locally run programmes of this kind. Indeed, colleges which have to date made use of this service favour its extension.

Management education and initial teacher training

A specific recommendation made in the ACSTT discussion document was that consideration be given to 'the possible inclusion of an element of introduction to administration and management at the initial teacher training stage' (ACSTT, 1978, p9). All heads of department were asked to comment on this proposal. Their responses indicated that they were equally divided as to whether such an 'element of introduction' would be appropriate at such an early stage in a teacher's career. There was some confusion over the failure of ACSTT to make clear what is meant by 'the initial teacher training stage' since in FE this could come at almost any time in a teacher's career. Respondents did, however, largely see this as referring to pre-service training.

Of those in favour of the proposal, less than ten per cent suggested that this introduction should be theoretical in nature. A slightly larger proportion suggested that a more appropriate preparation would include information on national, regional, local and college administrative and management structures; the organization and financ-ing of the FE sector; alternative college organizational structures, such as the matrix; the working and influence of Burnham; recent legislation, such as the Employment Protection Act; and the chain of decision-making and provision of resources from central to local government and so to the colleges. It was, however, stressed that 'any such component should be very basic and developed later when the teacher has found his or her feet'. By far the majority view among those favouring the ACSTT proposal was that any introduction should be at a purely practical level. The kind of items mentioned in this instance were referred to by some heads as 'essentially clerical work'; it was strongly believed that teachers did not welcome this kind of duty and often regarded it as 'someone else's job'. Above all it was stressed that 'staff should have a knowledge of the administration and management of colleges in order to give them a much better indication of their position in the total organiz-ation at an early stage in their careers'. Many junior staff agreed with the view that any introduction to administration and management should be essentially practical, since there is already a widespread feeling that teacher-training courses give too much emphasis to theory and too little to teaching problems and practices (see Chapter 7). Perhaps in the management area, too,

teachers would be more likely to see the relevance of
any theoretical framework once they had a certain amount
of practical experience on which to build.

A number of the heads who agreed that some preparation in
management and administration should be given before the
start of teaching employment, nevertheless suggested that
this would be most appropriate within the context of an
existing college induction course. Some argued that this
was in fact already in operation but reference to the
college induction programmes in question reveals in most
cases that any management component is a talk given by a
senior staff member on the workings of the local education
authority (see Chapter 6). One view expressed by heads
was that the content of any introductory course should
be 'specific to present college needs and to the administrative duties of the individual in his or her post'.
Clearly this would also necessitate provision on an in-
house in-service basis. In the larger colleges it was
suggested that there would be few difficulties in setting
up such a course of training. For smaller colleges, the
possibility existed of co-operating with other local
schools and colleges to offer a course for all new staff
at the beginning of each academic year.

Those who were not in favour of an early introduction to
administration and management were notably uniform in
their reasons for adopting this view. Among these heads
there was a common feeling that staff would obtain greater benefit from such training after a few years experience
in the FE system, and that teachers in training should
regard the development of classroom rather than administrative skills as their paramount objective.

The ACSTT discussion document gives no indication as to
who will be expected to 'give consideration to the possible inclusion of an element of introduction to administration and management'. Whether this should occur
during a Certificate in Education or CGLI 730 course or
during a local authority or college based induction course,
and what its exact nature should be are at present open
to question. If such an element is indeed included as
part of future formal training courses, FE managers
must ensure that it is built upon in a systematic way
throughout a teacher's career. Under the present system
it was suggested that any introduction to these skills
at the initial training stage would be wasted as the knowledge would soon be forgotten if it could not be used.

In-house training courses

Our inquiries suggest that there is widespread rejection
within institutions of the idea that management studies
departments can perform a valuable training function at
little cost. While many staff are quite prepared to
learn from management specialists operating from external
institutions, they refuse to concede that their own
colleagues may be in possession of a similarly useful
body of knowledge from which they may draw. This potential
for in-house provision is, then, invariably ignored while
vital financial and human resources are being expended in
releasing staff to attend external courses.

Three possible explanations were offered by staff we interviewed to account for this reluctance to accept internal provision as a viable possibility. The first centres
on the question of whether a fundamental difference exists
between the skills required for the control of industrial
or commercial organizations and those needed to ensure
the successful operation of an educational institution.
Proponents of this view argued that their needs were in-
trinsically different from those being met by their
colleagues who specialize in training managers for industry. Bailey (1977) has pointed to the paradox inherent
in a situation where further education has long been a
major provider for the training needs of industrial management, yet 'the management skills and techniques so respect-
ed by industry are not used to their fullest extent in
the management of the institutions from which they stem'
(p95). He argues that FE management should be of the
highest order unless there is in practical terms a fundamental difference between the skills required for the
control of industrial and commercial organizations and
those needed to ensure the effective operation of an
educational institution. Certainly the elements of
industrial management outlined in the related literature –
motivating, communicating, controlling, planning, organizing, and creating – do not appear out of place in an
educational context (Hicks and Gullett, 1976). Indeed
the ACSTT discussion document offers a definition which
implies a very similar view of the concept (ACSTT, 1978,
p4). Glatter (1972) moreover has argued that, 'It is
scarcely possible to conceive of administrative training (in education) without substantial borrowing from
studies of management in other contexts – particularly
the industrial, since this is where most research work
has been done'. Nevertheless, a number of staff in our
study colleges – and particularly those at more senior
levels – even went so far as to say that their needs
were specific to them as individuals in the context of

their present job. This inevitably led to the rejection
of external as well as internal expertise.

Secondly, we learned that senior staff often turned down
the opportunity to attend internally-run courses for fear
of losing some degree of credibility. Some suggested
that this problem might be overcome by arranging for
management studies specialists from one college to put on
courses for staff from other colleges in the locality:
'A sort of exchange of resources'. Whatever the validity
of the stance taken by senior staff, easily available
opportunities to acquire an introduction to the skills
of management and administration should be offered to
more junior staff. The third explanation lies in the
adage that the prophet is least honoured in his own land.
Staff rarely believe that their colleagues who specialize
in management studies have the necessary expertise to
offer them any real guidance. Where either of the latter
explanations is offered, it seems extremely unfortunate
that such potential for in-house provision is lost.
There are, of course, areas of training where regional
or national provision would be the most appropriate
solution; there are others in which in-house expertise
could perform a particularly useful function. In view of
the inadequacy of current training provision, colleges
must find alternative ways of approaching the question
of management training without total reliance on external
provision. Yet we could find very little evidence that
colleges were actually facing up to this challenge.

One of the colleges in our sample runs termly seminars
with papers being given by, for example, members of the
School of Business and Social Studies. Senior staff do
attend these and generally find them to be of value.
In another college a head of faculty reported that, in
order to help his heads of school and section to cope
with their managerial roles, he arranged management
seminars and short courses within the faculty. In two
of the colleges courses had been run in the past but had
been disbanded due to lack of interest.

On-the-job training.

The design and provision of appropriate courses are
obviously important elements in any planned training
programme for education management. Courses are not,
however, the only or even the most efficient way of
achieving the desired improvement in both the quality
and quantity of training provision at all levels. The
ACSTT discussion document remarked on 'the possibilities
of improving and developing management skills through the

186

normal work of the institution and the responsibilities
assigned to individual posts, and the contribution of
on-the-job learning. Jobs themselves should be organized
so as to broaden experience and knowledge' (ACSTT, 1978,
p8). Many senior staff argue that this is already common
practice within FE; others counter that the *ad hoc* distribution of administrative tasks is now being justified
after the event as on-the-job training.

As noted earlier, recent years have seen the increased
participation of relatively junior staff in decisions
which may have a fundamental effect on the policies and
procedures of the institutions in which they work. Such
developments require a fuller knowledge of planning and
organizational skills, and a greater awareness of management techniques on the part of the classroom teacher.
Systematic on-the-job training to meet these needs will
undoubtedly be looked upon with more favour as the demand
for training increases and financial resources diminish.
There is a still stronger argument to recommend this
approach: on-the-job experience, if properly supervised
and guided, can provide the logical progression through
a sequence of related administrative and managerial roles
which has always been lacking in the FE system. Recognizing this fact, individual institutions are beginning to
develop the administrative and managerial skills and
potentialities of their staff by providing them with
opportunities for involvement in the selection of new
staff members, job or task rotation, service on a wide
variety of working parties and committees, interdepart-
mental secondments, and other exercises which offer
teachers a broader view of the workings of their institution not normally encountered within a single department.

Colleges do, of course, vary enourmously in the range of
opportunities offered and in the extent to which these
form part of a systematic development plan. It should
also be said that staff themselves vary in the extent
to which they welcome the opportunity to take on administrative and managerial responsibilities. These are in
fact becoming increasingly unpopular among more junior
staff as the chance to allocate remission for such tasks
declines. In all of the colleges in our study the main
opportunity for staff to receive on-the-job training
in education management is through membership of the
Academic Board and a variety of decision-making
committees and working parties at both the college and
departmental levels. Heads of department see these as
useful in that 'they acquaint staff with a number of
management problems, such as costings and planning'. Of
those responding to the teachers' questionnaire 86 per

187

cent of principal lecturers, 65 per cent of senior
lecturers, 64 per cent of lecturers grade II and 42 per
cent of lecturers grade I reported that they were currently serving on at least one committee, working party or
examination board. In colleges with a large number of
committees, senior staff did, however, recognize that
staff were becoming increasingly unwilling to serve. If
staff are to be convinced that such activities have a
genuine place in any well-developed programme for enhancing skills, and the legitimacy of such an approach
is certainly not being questioned here, there is a need
for more systematic help and support for participation.
A view expressed on several occasions was that college
committee structures might function more effectively and
efficiently if all members and potential members of
committees had more expertise in this area.

In the questionnaire sent to staff below head of department level, one item asked for details of any experience
of carrying out management tasks respondents had had in
their present college. The question was deliberately
phrased in general terms, since its main purpose was to
discover those activities which staff themselves perceived as falling within the broad definition of 'management tasks'. Despite the fact that almost half of the
respondents (48 per cent) belonged to at least one
committee, working party or examination board, only five
per cent gave this as part of their response. Thus staff
do not generally regard this type of responsibility as
preparation for a management role.

A more common response (18 per cent) came from those who
saw their responsibilities as course tutors as involving
management tasks; while the highest positive response to
this question came from deputy heads of department, section
leaders and course co-ordinators. Thus staff were able to
assess the implications of this question as their role
within the management structure of their college became
more formally defined. A further 18 per cent of respondents listed a variety of additional tasks including timetabling, room allocation, record keeping, student enrolment
and similar items which are commonly regarded as falling
within the realm of administration rather than management.
It is, however, of importance to note that teachers may be
able to learn something of management and administration
from work undertaken outside their official college duties.
For instance, certain individuals stressed that they had
learned a great deal about management tasks from having
held positions in the college branch of NATFHE.

Finally, 13 per cent of the questionnaire respondents felt

that their work had offered them no opportunity, to date,
for gaining management experience - and this included
eight per cent of staff currently at senior lecturer
level.   The vast discrepancies between teachers' perceptions of what constitutes a management task are perhaps
most apparent in their comments: 'I am too busy teaching to get involved in such things': 'I am a teacher,
not a manager'; 'All teaching is management'.

The most important element of on-the-job training is the
notion of delegation. Makin (1979) describes this as
the 'lynch-pin of staff development' and points to the
potential pitfalls for senior staff who fail to give
sufficient priority to this aspect of their work. Heads
frequently claim that they have insufficient time to
stand back and reflect on their own practice. This surely
must point to a need for increased delegation to improve
the overall management strategy of a department. Where
teachers were offered ample opportunities to assist
senior staff in their department, they tended to feel
that this was an extremely useful form of training. They
were also less likely to criticise their more senior
colleagues, regarding them rather as a 'valuable model
to emulate'. Where real delegation was not practised
staff frequently complained about the amount of 'routine
administration' they were required to undertake, arguing
that much of this work could be carried out by clerical
staff leaving teachers with more time for lesson preparation or curriculum development work. The apparent paradox of these divergent viewpoints is explained in large
measure by the fact that teachers' perceptions differ
as to whether tasks of this nature are preparation for
a management role or simply unwanted administrative chores
which have been hurriedly passed down from above.

Job rotation was seen as one way of broadening the hori-
zons of the individual staff member, though many
colleges are for practical reasons unable to practice it
to any significant degree. Staff nevertheless saw advantages in this exercise. A frequent comment was that,
'People tend to become bogged down in their own particular
specialisms and never think about the wider departmental
and college issues'. One argument frequently brought
against the idea of rotation was that it would undermine
continuity. Those staff who were in favour of rotation
countered this by maintaining that the appointment of
deputies (who would eventually take over) effectively
prevents this from happening. In one college in our
sample all staff who take on additional responsibilities
are asked to try to involve 'understudies' as a matter
of policy. A similar system operates in one of the smaller

colleges in the sample where, if a head of department
is away, a senior lecturer is asked to deputize. There
are two senior lecturers in each department, and any
attempt to label either one of them as the 'deputy' is
officially discouraged. Heads in this as in other
colleges also expect their departmental staff to deputize
for them on external committees and working parties.

Overall the vast majority of heads of department in our
study colleges argued that their staff were provided
with at least some form of on-the-job training in administration and management. They were, however, divided
over how systematic such arrangements actually were. One
head of department frankly admitted of his own procedures
that, 'This tends to happen by accident rather than
design. Certainly opportunities are given, but not as
a planned exercise'. The time now seems ripe for senior
staff to consolidate the various practices in this area
into a systematic and planned programme of development.

Overview

The overriding concern about the development of staff
has focused on enhancing their skills as teachers, yet
the nature of the demands now being placed on the further
education manager has pointed to an urgent need for
improvement in the quality and quantity of relevant
training programmes. In an attempt to catch up with the
past the major impetus in this area is being directed
towards identifying the needs and planning appropriately
for staff at or above head of department as the first
recognized managerial grade. In the longer term, it is
hoped that education management training will come to be
centred on the idea of a career-long programme incorporating the necessary elements of preparation for a
variety of administrative and managerial roles.

Interviews with staff at all levels have suggested four
major managerial issues which need to be better understood
and in which staff feel there is distinct room for improvement: interpersonal relations and communication; decision
making structures and processes; delegation patterns and
techniques; and the management of financial resources.
It may be argued that such issues are of the essence in
any consideration of the managerial role. The effects of
the present economic climate mean for senior staff that
work in the areas of staff motivation and the establishment of incentives, interviewing, counselling and team
work are taking on an increasing importance. Because
democratization has made traditional managerial roles
less well defined, there is a common suspicion that the

leadership function is becoming undermined or even unnecessary. In reality, participative management requires
a new style of leadership based on a more sophisticated
knowledge of interpersonal relations. Our evidence would
indicate a growing need for training in all of these areas.

Current thinking among providing agencies at the regional
and local levels inclines towards offering a variety of
short courses. The great diversity which characterizes
FE institutions points above all to a need for flexibility
in the organization of such provision. Our findings
would suggest, for example, that attendance at a given
course should not be restricted to staff occupying a
particular grade but should be topic orientated. The
balance between theory and practice will also need to be
carefully considered, as will the nature of the theoretical
component itself. Much existing provision is organized
on the assumption that further education staff with management responsibilities have particular operational needs
arising from the context in which they work. This in
turn has led to a tendency to see FE in isolation from
the mainstream of management theory. In future it may
be expected that FE managers will be encouraged to develop
a broad-based critical understanding of management principles which will be of use to them in meeting new
situations.

The numbers of staff below head of department status who
have had the opportunity to attend any kind of course in
administration or management are exceedingly small.
Nevertheless developments arising from TEC, BEC, UVP and
YOP schemes and from the general move towards democratization necessitate a fuller knowledge of planning procedures
and organizational skills and a greater awareness of
management techniques in the part of the classroom teacher. Recognizing the fact that resources are unlikely to
permit formal management training for all stafff, at
least in the forseeable future, individual institutions
are beginning to develop the managerial skills and
potentialities of their staff by the use of on-the-job
training. The *ad hoc* delegation of unwanted administrative
tasks can play no part in such a scheme. Rather, such
informal training must be operated as a systematic programme of development facilitating a logical progression
through a series of related administrative and managerial
roles - something which has long been absent from the
further education scene.

Because of the need to ensure a more effective use of
resources it must be expected that efforts will be made
to overcome resistance to the idea of in-house management

courses. Self-help in the form of joint-college initiatives and informal discussion sessions are already achieving popularity, and Coombe Lodge staff are keen to offer advice and assistance to local and regional groups. It may indeed be the case that such co-operative ventures will characterize the future of management training in the further education sector.

CHAPTER 13

Discussion and recommendations

It is perhaps ironic that further education colleges,
which have for many years provided training for staff in
other sectors, have only relatively recently paid attention to formalizing training and development for their
own staff. Publications such as the ACSTT and ACFHE/APTI
reports were formulated during a period when student and
staff numbers had grown substantially, and there was concern to increase the number of trained teaching staff.
In the past few years radical changes in curricula and
in the student population have once again drawn attention
to the training needs of FE teachers. At the same time,
financial constraints have emphasized the need for the
efficient use of staff and for cost-effective development
programmes. It has been suggested that, because of decreased staff recruitment and promotion prospects, staff
development has a crucial role to play in motivating
and preparing staff to meet demands for different types
of course from a growing number of students. Moreover,
teachers may have to accept assessment for their own
benefit, and be prepared to sacrifice a week each year
of their own time for in-service training (Bevan, 1980).
Thus professional development could well become a con-
tractual obligation.

Our study indicates that such attitudes are still a long
way from being accepted by FE staff generally. Indeed,
in several colleges we visited in the exploratory phase
of the project, we formed the impression that some staff
have been frustrated in their efforts to increase current
development opportunities by the lack of interest shown
by the majority. As one vice-principal commented: 'I
see my task as trying to convince staff that development
is necessary at all. With no promotion prospects and
redundancy looming large, staff are simply keen to
survive as best they can. They see staff development

schemes as a luxury appropriate to better times'.

In such an atmosphere the introduction of successful
staff development schemes will depend less on the particular strategies adopted than on a rethinking of such
fundamental topics as the relation between development
and promotion, the assessment of college and of individual
needs and the funding of different types of development
activity. Without a reappraisal of such issues, development programmes may continue to be described as 'low
profile, don't make waves operations, feeling their way
in waters ranging from mildly supportive to downright
hostile' (Gross, 1977, p2). In addition to these wider
concerns, the size of college, the level of work predominantly taught, the number and types of departments
and the organizational structure and general climate all
influence the type of provision a college makes: they
help explain why the approach to staff development cannot
be identical in any two colleges. For this reason we
have not tried to provide a model of staff development
which colleges could emulate. Instead we have tried to
elicit general themes, which we hope will be of use to
colleges wishing to devise the staff development programme most appropriate to their particular situation.
We remain committed to the view that staff development
must be seen within its organizational context. To form-
ulate policies and subsequently to understand how in
practice they operate, a great deal needs to be known
about the internal dynamics of a college: 'Understand
the institution first;   then follow the path to development' (Hewton, 1980). Knowledge is required about informal networks and processes within the organization.
Unofficial leaders may in certain circumstances be more
influential than those with official status.   It cannot
be assumed that staff perceptions of objectives will be
congruent with those of management. Within the colleges,
however, internal conflict is commonly regarded as an
organizational problem;   a skeleton which keeps threatening to fall out of the cupboard. Seeking to confront
and overcome internal conflict must be seen as necessary
in order to alter structures, challenge traditional
beliefs and create an appropriate environment for a
workable staff development scheme to flourish. Often,
however, those involved in staff development are reticent
to enter this field of battle, fearing that the ground
gained in the past may be lost. Indeed, there is a tendency to adjust by daily reactions to immediate pressures.
The political dimension of staff development cannot be
ignored if it is to lose its marginal status and take a
central role in college life. Although the political
nature of the development enterprise is most

manifest in the competition for resources, there are
many other, but perhaps less easily identifiable points,
where the struggle for power occurs. Staff development
itself may become a focus for pre-existing tensions and
is not likely to work where the relationship between
management and staff, department and department, union
and management, college and LEA have become strained. In
such circumstances, barriers to the implementation of
policies will inevitably occur.

At the root of staff development is a concern for
educational standards in general and quality of teaching
in particular. We were not able, however, within the
confines of this study to investigate the effect staff
development may have upon student performance, attitudes
and motivation, if indeed this is possible. We have had
to assume that staff development will be ultimately to
their benefit, even if in the short term some students
may be taught by teachers whose attention may be in part
focused on their own studies.

Should staff development be formalized? It has been
suggested that 'organizations survive, and indeed sometimes flourish, in spite of (some might say because of!)
the lack of formal schemes of staff development' (Tolley,
1981, p3). Our study leads us to conclude that a formalized staff development scheme is more likely to be successful in involving all staff, especially in large colleges.
However, formal schemes will not succeed if they exist
only on paper; well-documented policy on staff development is worth little if management does not support it or
if junior staff are insufficiently well informed about
both college policy and the availability of development
opportunities.

Undoubtedly consideration of such broad themes and the
problems they pose is fundamental if staff development
programmes are to be successfully implemented. In
addition there are many more specific points which need
to be considered, and we have attempted to make recommendations which relate to particular aspects of staff development. We are well aware that recommendations have a
tendency to be criticized as too generalized, and in the
current financial climate, pleas for more resources for
remission from class contact are likely to be regarded
as unrealistic. However, many lecturers did feel that
staff development activities were becoming difficult to
pursue when they were increasingly expected to take on a
host of additional duties outside the classroom. It is
important that our recommendations are considered in the
context of the full report. They are not given in any

order of priority but, where possible, we have tried to separate those which are directed at colleges and at local education authorities, or are of national importance. Where ACSTT has made similar recommendations, this is noted.

Recommendations

1. College level

1.1 Detailed statements relating to the policy and practice of staff development should be drawn up and widely disseminated throughout the college.

1.2 A systematic two-way communication procedure should be established so that junior staff are aware of staff development opportunities and their views are considered by senior staff when staff development decisions are made.

1.3 The criteria for support for different types of staff development activity should be well publicized both by the LEA and the college.

1.4 One or more individuals should be made responsible for the collection and prompt dissemination of detailed information on courses and other development opportunities. For this purpose a bulletin should be circulated to all staff. In particular, existing schemes for industrial secondment and for overseas exchange and visits should be better publicized.

1.5 More effective procedures should be established for staff to report back to their colleagues on the content of courses and conferences they have attended. Mechanisms should also be introduced for overseas exchangees and staff who have participated in overseas exchanges and visits to inform college staff of other countries' educational policies and practices, especially their approaches to similar educational problems.

1.6 In policy statements particular attention should be given to: the roles and responsibilities of individuals; how staff development fits into the overall college plan; how priorities will be established and the formal application procedures.

1.7 Documentation relating to staff development should be subject to regular discussion and review.

1.8 Policy statements which include explicit reference to career advancement as a main aim of staff development should be amended. If modified to include mention of job enrichment, the term should be clarified.

1.9 Staff development requirements should be assessed in the light of performance.

1.10 Urgent attention should be paid to how performance and needs are to be evaluated, and staff at all levels should be consulted regarding the most appropriate means by which this might be achieved. Procedures employed should be formal and systematic: total reliance should not be placed on the self-identification of needs, and the opportunity should always be established for assessor and assessee to discuss assessment; interviews should be scheduled for this purpose.

1.11 Provision for counselling, especially career counselling, should be built into any assessment scheme.

1.12 As a prerequisite for introducing an assessment scheme, staff who will have major responsibility for its functioning should be trained in evaluation techniques and interviewing.

1.13 Job descriptions should be written for each member of staff. These should reflect the individual's own role and responsibilities within the college, and should be regularly discussed and updated.

1.14 Teachers should be positively encouraged to obtain feedback on their performance from colleagues and students.

1.15 Full-time professional tutor appointments should continue to be made and these should be established positions.

1.16 The main duties of a professional tutor should be clearly delineated.

1.17 All staff with major responsibility for staff development should be clearly identified; attention should be paid to their selection and training, and their duties clearly defined.

1.18 Appropriate induction programmes should be introduced for all teaching staff joining a college, irrespective of their previous training or experience. For both senior and junior staff such programmes should commence with a short *introduction* to college administrative procedures, personnel, formal and 'unwritten' regulations. This could take the form of a one- or two-day course with follow-up meetings later in the year. This should be followed by a formal induction to teaching (ACSTT 1 rec 1, 5-9).

1.19 (a) *College handbook:* A handbook giving details of college organization, personnel and procedures should supplement the introduction course.

(b) *Departmental information banks:* A bank of information containing details of timetables, past syllabuses and examinations would greatly help new staff.

1.20 *Mentor scheme:* A formal mentor scheme should be established for newly-appointed staff. Preferably mentors should be recently appointed lecturers at the same level as the new recruit, and they should receive remission and training for their work (particularly in counselling skills)(ACSTT 1 rec 5).

1.21 *Reduced load:* All junior lecturers new to FE should be given a reduced teaching load during their first year in addition to release to attend an induction programme. (ACSTT 1 rec 9(i))

1.22 (a) Induction programmes should take account of lecturers' differing levels of familiarity with educational theory and practice.

(b) Each induction programme should concentrate on practical problems facing lecturers in the classroom. (ACSTT 1 rec 12)

1.23 *Probationary year:* Lecturers should receive more guidance and feedback on their teaching during their first year of teaching. (ACSTT 1 rec 9(iii))

1.24 Lecturers should receive release from class contact to attend day-release courses, particularly in the first year of teaching.

1.25 Colleges, either jointly or individually, should offer an annual internal short-course programme which reflects staff training needs. Attention should be paid to the selection and training of course organizers and tutors.

1.26 Staff for whom research or consultancy is an appropriate form of development should be encouraged to engage in this activity regardless of the level of work taught or proportion of advanced level teaching carried out in their college.

1.27 Colleges should ensure a more effective use of in-house resources in creating a wider range of development experiences; for example, through inter-departmental secondments.

1.28 Most lecturers should have direct regular contact with industrial and commercial concerns.

1.29 Remission should be increased to enable lecturers to maintain regular contacts with local industry, commerce and the public service; release should also be made available for lecturers wishing to update their industrial work experience.

1.30 Overseas exchanges and visits should have full recognition as a valuable form of staff development.

1.31 Where private arrangements are made, these should be formalized to ensure that lecturers are not disadvantaged on their return; for example, regarding pension rights.

1.32 The duties of those members of staff directly involved in the administration of these schemes should be delineated.

1.33 Time and support should be made available to all staff involved in new work, both for the preparation of courses and their subsequent development and revision.

1.34 Staff development schemes should include provision for training in the skills of management and administration.

1.35 Planning for education management training should be centred on the idea of a career-long programme incorporating relevant elements of preparation for a variety of administrative and managerial roles.

1.36 Short management courses should be topic rather than grade orientated.

1.37 In planning management training courses greater advantage should be taken of existing in-house expertise.

1.38 Self-help in the form of joint-college initiatives should be encouraged.

1.39 A systematic programme of on-the-job training in administration and management should be introduced to facilitate a logical progression through a series of related managerial and administrative roles.

2.   National and local authority level

2.1   (a) The various schemes of initial training should be combined and rationalized to avoid repetition when lecturers take a full certificate course. (ACSTT 1 rec 17-19)

      (b) The current range of training modes (day-release full and part-time) should remain, and lecturers should be given more freedom to choose a particular training course and mode to suit individual circumstances.

(c) Initial teacher-training courses should take account of lecturers' differing levels of familiarity with educational theory and practice.

(d) There should be more emphasis in these courses on practical teaching problems and on motivating students.

(e) Tutors responsible for teacher-training should have up-to-date FE teaching experience. Joint appointments (college/college of education) or secondments and exchanges could achieve this.

(f) Assessment procedures on initial training courses should be reviewed.

2.2   Post-experience training and development should be awarded equal priority with initial teacher-training, and this should be reflected in resource allocation.

2.3   *Secondment:* to industry, commerce or the public service for periods of a term or a year should become more common and given as high a priority as release to pursue higher qualifications. The regulations giverning release for course attendance should be modified to include release for industrial secondment. A greater variety of employers should be encouraged to become involved in such schemes.

2.4   (a) The introduction of any new work requiring curriculum development must be planned well ahead of implementation so that the development needs of staff can be assessed in good time.

(b) Lecturers should receive more training in skills relevant to curriculum development – initial teacher-training and management courses could cover aspects of this work.

2.5   Guidelines should be produced regarding the terms professional tutor and staff development officer and their usage.

2.6   All professional tutors should be trained (ACSTT 1 rec24) especially in the areas of inter-personal skills, conflict management and counselling.

Appendix

a) References

ADVISORY COMMITTEE ON THE SUPPLY AND TRAINING OF TEACHERS:
FE SUB-COMMITTEE (1975). *The Training of Teachers for
Further Education.* (Haycocks Report)

ADVISORY COMMITTEE ON THE SUPPLY AND TRAINING OF TEACHERS:
FE SUB-COMMITTEE (1978). *The Training of Adult
Education and Part-Time Further Education Teachers.*
ACSTT Discussion paper.

ADVISORY COMMITTEE ON THE SUPPLY AND TRAINING OF TEACHERS:
FE SUB-COMMITTEE (1978). *Training Teachers for
Educational Management in Further and Adult Education.*
ACSTT Discussion paper.

ASSOCIATION OF COLLEGES OF FURTHER AND HIGHER EDUCATION/
ASSOCIATION OF PRINCIPALS IN COLLEGES (1973). *Staff
Development in Further Education.* London:ACFHE/APC.

ASTLE, T. (1980). 'The Education and Training of the
"Holland" Student'. In: HERBERT, R.H. ed. *Extended
Roles of the Colleges of FE,* 7-10. W. Midlands Council
for FE.

AUSTIN, E. (1975). 'The role of the teacher-tutor.'
Ideas, 30, Jan., 222-6.

BACON, F. (1972). 'Report or support?' *The Technical
Journal, 10,* 2, 15-16.

BAILEY, R. (1977). 'Management of education - an industrial
comparison', *J. of F. and H.Educ., 1,3,* 94-105.

BEVAN, J. (1980). *T.E.S.,* 7.11.80.

BIRCH, R. (1977). *Evaluating the Effectiveness and
Efficiency of Coombe Lodge.* Coombe Lodge policy paper.

BOLAM, R. (1977). 'Training the trainers', *Trends,3,*21-6.

BRADLEY, J. and SILVERLEAF, J. (1979). *Making the Grade:
Careers in FE Teaching.* Windsor:NFER.

BRIAULT, E.W.H. (1973). 'Staff Development in the institutional setting'. In: PRATT, S. ed. *Staff Development in Education.* London: Councils of Educ. Press.

CANTOR, L.M. and ROBERTS, I.F. (1979). *Further Education: A Critical Review*. London: Routledge & Kegan Paul.

COLES, C.F. (1977). 'Developing Professionalism: Staff Development as an Outcome of Curriculum Development', *Programmed Learning and Educ. Tech.*, *14*,4,315-8.

COUNCIL FOR NATIONAL ACADEMIC AWARDS (1973). *Report of the Working Party on Resources for Research in Polytechnics and Other Colleges*, London:CNAA.

DAVEY, H. (1976). 'The staff tutor's work', *Secondary Education*, *6*, 2,9-10.

DAVIES, H. and TAUSSIK, T. (1980). 'Staff development and the role of the head of department', *NASD J.*,*3*,12-17.

DEPARTMENT OF EDUCATION AND SCIENCE (1969). *Report of the Committee on Technician Courses and Examinations* (Haslegrave Report) London: HMSO.

DEPARTMENT OF EDUCATION AND SCIENCE (1970). *Government and Conduct of Establishments of Further Education*. (Circular 7/70).

DEPARTMENT OF EDUCATION AND SCIENCE (1970). Administrative Memos 14/70 and 26/70.

DEPARTMENT OF EDUCATION AND SCIENCE (1972). *Education: A Framework for Expansion*. London:HMSO.

DEPARTMENT OF EDUCATION AND SCIENCE (1972). *Teacher Education and Training*. (James Report). London:HMSO.

DEPARTMENT OF EDUCATION AND SCIENCE (1976). *Report by H.M. Inspectors on Curricula for Non-Participant 16-19s*. (Sundale Report). London:HMSO.

DEPARTMENT OF EDUCATION AND SCIENCE (1977). *The Training of Teachers for Further Education*. (Circular 11/77).

DEPARTMENT OF EDUCATION AND SCIENCE (1978). *Report of the Committee of Enquiry into the Education of Handicapped Children and Young People*. (Warnock Report). London:HMSO.

DES, SCOTTISH EDUCATION DEPT. WELSH OFFICE AND DEPTS. OF EMPLOYMENT AND INDUSTRY (1979). *A Better Start in Working Life. Vocational Preparation for Employed Young People in Great Britain*. A consultative paper.

EBBUT, K. and BROWN, R. (1978). 'The structure of power in the FE college', *J. of F. and H. Educ.*,2,3.

ELTON, L. and SIMMONDS, K. (1976). *Staff development in higher education*. Guildford:SRHE.

ERAUT, M., CONNORS, B. and HEWTON, E. (1980). *Training in Curriculum Development and Educational Technology in Higher Education*. London:Society for Research into Higher Education Monograph.

FURTHER EDUCATION STAFF COLLEGE (1971-76). *College Management readings and cases, vols 1-5*. A Staff Development Handbook.

FURTHER EDUCATION CURRICULUM REVIEW AND DEVELOPMENT UNIT (1978). *Experience Reflection Learning: suggestions for organizers of schemes of UVP*. London:F.E.U.

GLATTER, R. (1972). *Management Development for the Education Profession*. London:Harrap.

GLEESON, D. and MARDLE, G. (1980). *Further Education or Training? A Case Study in the Theory and Practice of Day-release Education*. London:Routledge & Kegan Paul.

GRAY, H.L. (1979). 'Staff counselling in education'. *J. of F. and H. Educ.*, *3*, 1, 75-81.

GREENAWAY, H. and HARDING, A.G. (1978). *The Growth of Policies for Staff Development*. Monograph 34, London: Society for Research into Higher Education.

HARDING, B., McCALLUM, D.I. and ROBBINS, D. (1977). 'New Entrants into higher and further education teaching', *Brit. J. In-service Educ.*, *3*, 3, 220-8.

HEWTON, E. (1979a). 'A Strategy for Promoting Curriculum Development in Universities', *Studies in H.E.*,*4*,1,67-75.

HEWTON, E. (1979b). 'Towards a definition of staff development', *Impetus*, *2*, 1-8.

HEWTON, E. (1980). 'The Twilight World of Staff Development', *Studies in H.E.*, *5*, 2, 205-15.

HICKS, H.G. and GULLETT, C.R. (1976). *The Management of Organizations*. New York:McGraw-Hill.

HOPSON, B. (1973). 'Career Development in Industry: the Diary of an Experiment', *Brit. J. of Guidance and Counselling*, *1*, 1, 51-61.

HOTEL AND CATERING INDUSTRY TRAINING BOARD (1978). *Setting up UVP schemes. Guidelines for HCITB staff.*

HUMPHRIES, M., McALLISTER, M., OLIVER, D. and OSBORNE, P. (1980). *Loud and Clear? Summary of a study of Curriculum Dissemination in Further and Higher Education*. London: F.E.U.

JAMIESON WRAY, M., MOOR, C. and HILL, S. (1980). *Unified Vocational Preparation: an evaluation of the pilot programme*. Windsor: NFER.

JOINT ADVISORY COMMITTEE ON TEACHER EXCHANGE (1977). *Working Party Report to DES on the development of teacher exchange schemes.*

JONES, P., HOLLINSHEAD, B. and YORKE, M. (1980). *Designs for Teaching: an evaluation*. (C.E.T. sponsored project). Staff Development and Educational Methods Units, Manchester Polytechnic.

LODGE, B. (1980). 'Better by half'. *T.E.S.* 11.7.80.

MAKIN, J.P. (1979). 'Staff development in further education colleges'. In: *Staff Development*, Coombe Lodge Report, *12*, 10, 479-86.

MANPOWER SERVICES COMMISSION (1977). *Young people and work*. Report on the feasibility of a new programme of opportunities for unemployed young people. (Holland Report) London:M.S.C.

MARSH, D. (1979). 'Staff development: principles and practice'. In: *Staff Development*, Coombe Lodge Report, *12*, 10, 461-4.

MAW, B.J. (1975). 'Professional tutor or teacher tutor: what's in a name?', *Brit. J. In-service Educ.*,*2*,11-18.

MILLER, G. (1974). *Staff Development Programme in British Universities and Polytechnics*. International Institute for Educational Planning, Paris (IIEP mimeo.)

NATIONAL ASSOCIATION FOR STAFF DEVELOPMENT IN FURTHER AND HIGHER EDUCATION (1978). *A Commentary on the ACSTT Report regarding the Training of Full-time Teachers for Further Education*. NASD (mimeo.)

NATIONAL ASSOCIATION FOR STAFF DEVELOPMENT IN FURTHER AND HIGHER EDUCATION (1979). *A Commentary on the ACSTT Report regarding Training Teachers for Educational Management in Further and Adult Education*, NASD (mimeo.)

NATIONAL ASSOCIATION OF TEACHERS IN FURTHER AND HIGHER EDUCATION (1978). *The Education and Training of Teachers for Further and Higher Education. A Policy Statement*. London:NATFHE.

NORTH WESTERN REGIONAL ADVISORY COUNCIL FOR FURTHER EDUCATION STAFF DEVELOPMENT PROJECT, (1979). *Report of a study group on 'The Induction of New Staff'*, NWRAC.

OWEN, J.C. (1968). 'Strategies of curriculum innovation', *J. of Curriculum Studies*, *1*, 1.

OWEN, R.E. (1979). 'The changing role of the lecturer in further education', *Brit. J. In-service Educ.*.*5*,2,45-8.

OXTOBY, R. (1979). 'Problems facing heads of department', *J. of F. and H. Educ.*, *3*, 1, 46-59.

PANCKHURST, J. (1980). *Focus on Physical Handicap*. Windsor: NFER.

REGIONAL ADVISORY FOR THE ORGANIZATION OF FURTHER EDUCATION IN THE EAST MIDLANDS (1975). *Training and Development for F.E. Teaching Staff*. A report of the Advisory Panel for the training and development of F.E. teaching staffs. October.

RUSSELL, R. (1977). *The Curriculum Development Workshops at Coombe Lodge*. Coombe Lodge Working Paper.

RUSSELL, R. (1980). *A Review of the major styles of Curriculum Design in Further Education*, *1*, London:F.E.U.

SAYER, S. and HARDING, A. (1974). 'Time to look beyond technology to better use of human resources'.*THES*,20 Dec.

SCHON, D.A. (1971). *Beyond the Stable State*. London: Temple Smith.

SOFER, C. (1974). 'Social control in organizations with special reference to appraisal schemes'. In: TILLEY, K.W. ed. *Leadership and Management*, 3-26. London: The English University Press.

SOUTHERN NETWORK (1977). Staff Development Newsletter, Number 1, February.

TAYLOR, P. (1977). 'Evaluating in-service programmes', *Trends in Education*, *3*, (Aut.) 6-11.

TAYLOR, W. (1978a) 'The value of in-service training', *THES*, 11.8.81.

TAYLOR, W. (1978b). *Research and reform in Teacher Education. European Trend Reports in Educational Research.* Windsor:NFER

THOMAS, K. and LEVINE, K. (1979). 'What progress towards college democracy? *NATFHE J.*, October, 10–11.

TEATHER, D.C.B. (1979). *Staff Development in Higher Education: an International review and bibliography,* London: Kogan Page.

TOLLEY, G. (1971). *Staff Development in Further Education.* London:ACFHE.

TOLLEY, G. (1981). *Staff Development in Further Education: Retrospect and Prospect.* London:ACFHE.

TRAINING SERVICES AGENCY (1975). *Vocational Preparation for Young People: a discussion paper.*

WAITT, I. (1980) ed. *College Administration: a Handbook.* London:NATFHE.

WALKER, M.P. (1978). 'The role and function of the professional tutor'. *APT Comment,* March, 1–12.

WARREN PIPER, D. (1975). 'The Longer Reach'. In: *Issues in Staff Development.* London:SDU/UTMU.

WARREN PIPER, D. and GLATTER, R. (1977). *The Changing University: a report on staff development in universities.* Windsor: NFER.

WATKINS, R. (1973) ed. *In-service training: Structure and Content.* London: Ward Lock.

WEST MIDLANDS REGIONAL CURRICULUM UNIT (1980). *YOP Survey.* FEU and West Midlands Advisory Council for FE.

WHEELER, G.E. (1977). *Management of a Further Education College.* London:ACFHE.

WHEELER, G.E. (1978). *The Further Education Staff College and Management In and Out of Education.* Coombe Lodge Report.

WILLIS JACKSON REPORT (1957). *The Supply and Training of Teachers for Technical Colleges.* London:HMSO.

YORKE, M. (1977). 'Staff development in further and higher education: a review'. *Brit. J. of Teacher Educ.*, *3*, 2, 161–8.

(b)   Useful names and addresses

The Association of Professional Tutors (APT)
Secretary: P Davison, Willesden College of Technology,
Denzil Road, London NW10 2DX

British Educational Research Association (BERA)
Secretary: P Chambers, Bradford College, Great
Horton Road, Bradford BD7 1AY

Business Education Council (BEC)
76 Portland Place, London W1N 4AA

Central Bureau for Educational Visits and Exchanges
43 Dorset Street, London W1H 3FN

City and Guilds of London Institute
76 Portland Place, London W1N 4AA

College of Preceptors
130 High Holborn, London WC1V 6PS

Council for Educational Technology (CET)
3 Devonshire Street, London W1N 2BA

Council for National Academic Awards
344-354 Gray's Inn Road, London WC1X 8BP

Further Education Curriculum Review and Development
   Unit (FEU)
Elizabeth House, York Road, London SE1 7PH

Further Education Research Association (FERA)
Secretary: A Bullock, Southgate Technical College,
High Street, London N14 6BS

Further Education Research Association (Northern
   Branch)
Secretary: F Lund, Bolton Institute of Technology,
Deane Road, Bolton BL3 2AB

Further Education Staff College (Coombe Lodge)
Blagdon, Bristol BS1 6RG

League for the Exchange of Commonwealth Teachers
Old Marshall House, 124 Belgrave Road, London SW1V 2BL

Manpower Services Commission (MSC)
Selkirk House, 166 High Holborn, London WC1V 6PF

National Association for Staff Development (NASD)
Secretary: F Bacon, Redgrave House, Prestbury,
Macclesfield SK10 4BW

National Association of Teachers in Further and
   Higher Education (NATFHE)
Hamilton House, Mabledon Place, London WC1H 9BH

National Bureau for Handicapped Students
C/o Middlesex Polytechnic, All Saints site,
White Hart Lane, London N17 8HR

Regional Advisory Councils:

London Home Counties Regional Advisory Council
for Technological Education, Tavistock House
South, Tavistock Square, London WC1H 9LR

Southern Regional Council for Further Education,
26 Bath Road, Reading RG1 6NT

Regional Council for Further Education in the
South West, 37-38 Fore Street, Taunton, Somerset,
TA1 1HR

West Midlands Advisory Council for Further
Education, Norfolk House, Smallbrook Queensway,
Birmingham B5 4NB

Regional Advisory Council for the Organisation
of Further Education in the East Midlands
Robins Wood House, Robins Wood Road, Aspley,
Nottingham NG8 3NH

East Anglian Regional Advisory Council for Further
Education, Shirehall, Bury St Edmunds, Suffolk,
IP33 2AN

Yorkshire and Humberside Council for Further
Education, Bowling Green Terrace, Leeds LS11 9SX

North Western Regional Advisory Council for
Further Education, Town Hall, Walkden Road,
Worsley, Manchester M28 4QE

Northern Advisory Council for Further Education,
5 Grosvenor Villas, Grosvenor Road, Newcastle-
upon-Tyne, NE2 2RU

Welsh Joint Education Committee, 245 Western
Avenue, Cardiff CF5 2YX

Royal Society of Arts (RSA)
6-8 John Adam Street, Adelphi, London WC2N 6EZ

Southern Science and Technology Forum
The Director: R H Gammon, The University,
Southampton SO9 5NH

Southern Staff Development Network
C/o J Haigh, Southgate Technical College, High Street
London N14 6BS

Standing Conference on Educational Development
Services in Polytechnics (SCEDSIP)
Secretary: R Fothergill, PETRAS, Newcastle-upon-Tyne
Polytechnic, Pandon Street, Newcastle-upon-Tyne

Technician Education Council (TEC)
76 Portland Place, London W1N 4AA

Understanding British Industry (UBI)
Sun Alliance House, New Inn Hall Street, Oxford,
OX1 2QE